Speak Up, Speak Out and Be Heard

How to Protest and Make It Count

Jeremy Holcomb

Loompanics Unlimited
Port Townsend, Washington

Neither the author nor the publisher assumes any responsibility for the use or misuse of information contained in this book. It is sold for informational purposes only. Be Warned!

Speak Up, Speak Out and Be Heard
How to Protest and Make It Count

© 2003 by Jeremy Holcomb

Cover by Craig Howell
Interior illustrations by Bob Crabb

Published by:
Loompanics Unlimited
PO Box 1197
Port Townsend, WA 98368
Loompanics Unlimited is a division of Loompanics Enterprises, Inc.
Phone: 360-385-2230
E-mail: service@loompanics.com
Web site: www.loompanics.com

ISBN 1-55950-238-X
Library of Congress Card Catalog Number 2003106877

Contents

Introduction 1

Chapter One 3
Who Cares? or The Only Two Problems in the World

Chapter Two 7
What Are Protests? or Why Am I Holding This Sign in the Rain?

Chapter Three 15
Players in a Protest

Chapter Four 23
The Importance of Having Clear Goals

Chapter Five 27
Protest Highlight: Marches

Chapter Six 45
Protest Highlight: Pickets

Chapter Seven 57
Protest Highlight: Blockades

Chapter Eight 71
Protest Highlight: Letter Campaigns

Chapter Nine 85
Protest Highlight: Boycotts

Chapter Ten 97
A Sample Protest

Chapter Eleven 105
Stories from the Trenches: Personal Experiences in Protests

Chapter Twelve 113
Advanced Tips and Tricks: Strategy and Tactics for Protest Success,
and Scarier Ways You Can Be Fucked With

Chapter Thirteen.. 131
Tools of the Trade: How to Build Your Protest Survival Pack

Chapter Fourteen 137
Getting Your Act Together: Working With a Group
or Starting Your Own

Chapter Fifteen.. 143
Alternatives to Protest

Chapter Sixteen 149
How to Make a Protest Sign

Chapter Seventeen.. 155
Personal Risk Assessment

Chapter Eighteen 159
Spin Control: How to Deal Effectively with the Media

Chapter Nineteen.. 165
Paying for It: Fundraising and Resources for Your Protests

Chapter Twenty 169
Things that Hurt Protests

Chapter Twenty-One 177
With Friends Like These…: Zealots and the Over-committed
on Your Own Side

Chapter Twenty-Two 183
Your Rights and the Powers of the Police
or So Now We Are Going to Jail

Chapter Twenty-Three 193
Protesting in 24 Hours or Less

The End? 199

Introduction

This is a book about conflict, about change. About the need to think about how we want the world to look, and then planning the action needed to bring that world into being. It is not about making you angry, but about channeling your anger, your desire, and your drive for a better world. Whether the goal is something as global as fighting for world peace, or something as close to home as getting the pot holes in your road paved, this book provides the tools and resources to plan and organize protests, to create change, and to help bring about the world you want to live in.

2

Here you can find strategy and tactics to organize protests of all types, and find the method of protest most suited to your needs. No matter what, your willingness to accept risk, to create conflict, to anger others may get the results you want. If you care enough, you can create change.

In addition to providing a close look at traditional protest methods (marches, boycotts, and so on), there are chapters on the police, protest support, and many of the secondary issues that every protest organizer should be aware of. By being aware of these issues, and having them in mind as you plan protests, you can put on better, more effective protests.

In the end, only you know what change you want, and only you can create that change. Here are some tools to help you do so.

Chapter One
Who Cares?
or
The Only Two Problems in the World

Every day thousands of issues and events touch our lives. Many touch us directly in a negative way. Many more touch us discreetly, making our lives less rich and fulfilling than they could be. One way to define a person is by what pisses

4

them off. Everyone, if pressed hard enough, can find things that piss them off, ways the world should be different, or things that must change. The issues are as diverse as the people involved. It could be anything, from abortion to zoo management, but there are thousands of them.

That said, there are really only two problems in the world. They are:

1. Not enough people are angry.

2. Not enough people explore how to be angry constructively.

People are, by nature, unwilling to confront the status quo. Things are the way they are. This is how it's always been done. My parents did it, I did it, and you'll do it. Don't rock the boat.

Being mad is hard. Anger is hard. Maintaining anger long enough to do something about it is even harder. It's easy to say that there is too much traffic on the road, but getting a lobbying effort for more buses takes work, and actually going to the governor's house and picketing takes not only work but a willingness to be confrontational. Not everyone starts out ready for this sort of thing, but if pushed far enough anyone can get there.

The Give Five Campaign suggests that you donate five hours a week to a cause you believe in. This is a solid goal, but I argue that it is ahead of its time. First, every member of a democratic society should spend one hour a week exploring things that piss them off. It is easy to say, "Yes, I'd like to protect the environment; I'd like a shorter commute; I'd like fewer nuclear weapons," but if the issue doesn't piss you off, it is not your issue.

Of course, if you're reading this, you probably already have your issue. Just realize that others may not have found theirs, or may not have your issue. Helping people become aware of and connect to your issue can be the fastest way to find allies for your cause.

Once people know what they care about, the goal is to act on it and get things done. You should protest either as a last resort, after everything else fails to work, or as part of a larger campaign to create change, but either way if you are going to protest, if you care enough to go out and fight (one way or another) for what you believe in, then you owe it to your cause to do it well.

This is not intended as a definitive work on the history, purpose, and social effect of protests, nor is this an ivory tower "this is the way it is" tome. This is a how-to book, an aid in helping you plan, stage, and deliver the protest most effective for your cause and get the results you want. Protest without thought is spit in the wind, and can be worse than doing nothing. Well thought out, well planned, and well-executed protest can and does change the world.

Protests have value because they work. Without social protest, without people mad enough to get up and march, write, and fight for what they believe in, women would not be voting, gays would be in hiding (or dead), and everyone whose skin isn't pale would be shit outta luck. Every act of protest, from thousands of people in the street to one person and one bus seat, has impact. Protest because you care. Protest because it works.

Good luck, and stay pissed off.

Chapter Two
What are Protests?
or
Why Am I Holding This Sign in the Rain?

The term "protest" covers a lot of ground. It is everything from strikes and picket lines to marching in the streets to lighting bulldozers on fire and sitting on platforms in a tree. But no matter what the act, protest is about communicating your ideas and goals. Protest, in essence, is communication to create change — change of opinion, of policy, of action. That communication may be with your target to demand change, with the public to raise awareness, or with third parties such as politicians to pass relevant laws, but the act of your protest should communicate your message.

In order to protest effectively you need to understand how to communicate your message to your advantage. Protest in a void is pointless. Worse, it is a loss of energy that could be directed to create meaningful change.

There are hundreds of ways to protest, from marching on Washington to a simple phone call. In order to constructively discuss protests, and assist you in running yours, protests can be grouped into one of three categories. Protests can be visible and cooperative, visible and antagonistic, or covert. The distinction is important to determine how you want to protest, what resources you need, what level and type of risk you will have, and to help plan the details of what you need to do.

Visible and Cooperative

This is a protest where you have the consent of at least some of the other parties involved, whether in the form of city permits for a march or administrative permission for a sit-in.

Advantages:

Improved media perception. If you go through the "official" channels to get your protest set up, the media tends to supply more favorable coverage. Whereas they might describe a group of people marching impromptu with no permit as "rabble rousers" or "dissidents," with a permit you become "activists." Since your overall goal will frequently be to shape public opinion, anything you can do to improve your media image will help.

Additional logistic and management support. Getting a thousand people together for a rally is great, but if you can get the city to set up a few porta-potties you can rally far longer.

Less interference from authority. By letting the powers that be have their say before you protest, you lower the likelihood that the cops/administration/people in charge will show up trying to arrest, disperse or provoke you. Getting your message out is one thing, but if the cops are arresting everyone who goes to the podium, it'll be a short speech.

Disadvantages:

Time. Going through the official channels takes time, often lots of it. Getting permits, submitting event plans, pleading your case, all this takes time away from the protest itself. In addition, for highly time-sensitive protests there may simply not be time to get permission. If you want to protest low teacher salaries you can plan ahead to do so near the start of the school year or budget season, and get the permits you need. If you want to protest the war the U.S. has suddenly gotten into and want to march in the streets immediately, getting permission may simply not be an option.

Outside control. If you rely on any outside body for permission to protest, you risk having them try to shape your message. A city planning office that decides to let you march but in a lower traffic area of town, or will let you set up a table but not post signs, is lowering the impact you can have. They may have perfectly legitimate reasons for wishing to do this, but the effect is the same. You should be aware that the powers that be may not wish your protest to go well, and adding so many restrictions to it that it collapses under its own weight is a much more effective (and legal) way to kill a protest than banning it outright. (Expect this kind of last minute change to official policy. It is becoming more and more common as a way to shut down protests.) Always fight to make sure the core elements you need for a protest are not tampered with, and always feel free to sue (or use other legal action) to get what you need.

Credibility. This isn't a huge issue, but under some circumstances getting advanced permission to protest may hurt the credibility of your message. For example, if you want to protest a university administrations policy on posting signs on campus, getting their permission to post signs might seem a bit hypocritical.

Media complacency. In media markets that have historically seen protests on a regular basis the media may be less willing to devote limited resources to covering a "peaceful" approved protest. Fifty people marching through Boise, Idaho, may be a huge story, but the same march on the streets of Seattle, Washington, won't even merit a reporter, let alone a camera crew.

Visible and cooperative protest examples:

- Parades on city streets with city permits
- Picketing public town meetings to protest a visiting politician
- Sidewalk information tables on public streets

Visible and Antagonistic

This is what more people think of as the "classic" protest, where your goal is to get out there and get your message to as many people as possible, regardless of the wishes of anyone else. From the anti-war march in the streets to sitting and blockading the doors of a government building to picketing a chemical company's animal testing, this is where you show the world that you are willing to fight for your cause even in the face of clear adversity.

Advantages:

Speed. Because you aren't relying on anything other than your own plans you can get a protest off the ground in the shortest time possible. As shown above, this may be the only option for time-sensitive subjects.

Flexibility. Since you aren't relying on anyone else for permission you are free to protest in the way you find most effective. From posting signs on telephone booths to blocking traffic, you can get your message out as directly as possible.

Media response. Unlike "permitted" protests, the conflict involved in bucking the system to get your message out almost guarantees that you will get the attention, and coverage of the media. It cannot be stressed enough how important this is, as the media will usually prove your main vehicle for getting your message to the public. One hundred people a day might see a picket sign. That same sign on the nightly news could reach 100,000 or more.

Disadvantages:

Spin. By going outside the "system" you invite the media, and to an extent the public, to brand you as a radical fringe that might be interesting or scary, but who can be ignored as fringe lunatics. The country as a whole may have become more tolerant of protests since the 1960s, but any time you block traffic to protest for cars with higher gas mileage there will always be people in SUVs who will just want to run you over.

Conflict. Protests are based on conflict (if you don't care enough to create conflict, don't protest) but if you antagonize people they are more likely to push back. Police who might just direct traffic and make people clean up after themselves at an unapproved protest may come to an unplanned march in riot gear. There are few things as intimidating as a wall of cops in riot gear with bright orange shotguns and an armored personnel carrier.

Visible and antagonistic protest examples:

- Marches in the streets with no permits
- Bicycle ride down the freeway to stall traffic
- Teach-ins inside campus facilities
- Blockades of office buildings

Covert Protests

Most protests try to change the world by influencing public opinion. They try to get people to vote a certain way, buy or not buy a product, or call their congressman. But sometimes the way you want to protest is to take the debate to the target in a more direct way. In the interest of staying out of prison, the author would like to point out that this is not an endorsement of this tactic, but it is important to understand what is going on out there.

The key difference between these and overt protests is visibility. Most of the time you want as much publicity as you can get, with the media, the public, and everyone else aware of what you're doing and why. With covert protests you want to stay out of sight, at least until you're done, to cover yourself.

This type of protest includes acts that go beyond being antagonistic into the blatantly illegal.

Why go this route? Most corporations are not evil, just profit driven. For the most part you don't spike trees, break into labs, or blow stuff up for the PR, you do it to change the profit equation the target is using and try to get them to change their ways. As the saying goes, those factories don't burn themselves down. No CEO decides to cut down an old growth forest because he hates trees; he does it because it makes him money. If you disrupt the process by going and torching his bulldozers you change that profit equation. Anybody even thinking of going this route should read the sections on violence and risk tolerance.

Advantages:

Direct effect. Corporations may not respond to letters, calls, and requests for change, but once you start to affect the bottom line you can pretty much be sure they'll pay attention (not that that's always good).

Disadvantages:

Image. The media is almost certain to give you negative coverage if/when your actions get out, and the public (which might support a march or rally) is much less likely to support violent action. People will support an activist far more than a terrorist, even if the titles cloak similar action.

Jail time. Check out the risk tolerance section. If you can't take the heat, stay out of the streets.

By knowing what category sounds best for your needs you can select the protest style that will best suit your needs, select the level of risk you are willing to take (and ask others to take), and set up and plan a successful protest.

Chapter 3
Players in a Protest

Every player in a protest comes to the table with different goals and expectations. By understanding what each of these parties wants, you can be more effective in meeting your own goals and creating the change you want.

You

You may be a large organization in your own right or just a few people, but your first step should be to understand your own capabilities. Understand the personnel, skills, and dedication you bring to your protest. If you only have three people to work with, don't plan a 1,000-person march. If you know nothing about writing, don't set out to send flyers to everyone. If you have never organized a protest and don't have much experience with organizing them don't try to set up the next Million Man March. Match your plans to your skills, and keep looking at ways you can train to meet additional needs.

Example: Dan is part of a student organization (at a large public university) devoted to protecting the environment. The city government has recently cut funds to a recycling program, and the group wants to express its displeasure with a protest. At this step they look at the group itself. They have eight full-time dedicated members and several hangers on, and access to the computers and resources of the university. They decide to explore holding a small march from the campus to the city government offices, picking up litter on the way to drop on the steps of city hall to show the need for recycling programs.

Goal: List your goals and capabilities. Know yourself, what you can do, and more importantly what you can't do by yourself. Use this information to decide what kind of protest you want to run.

Other Like-minded Organizations

Odds are, if something pisses you off, it pisses others off as well. You don't need to do everything yourself, and odds are you shouldn't try. As soon as you find the things you want to change, do some research into what other organizations exist that also fight for your cause. You may want to join them, or just ally with them when it suits you, but know who your friends are and what they do. The Web will provide most of your information on like-minded groups, and you can also find good information by asking organizations you've already found, and hitting the library for books on your topic and checking the bibliography and authors. Look at the chapter in this book on forming or joining a group for more on this important decision. It is also helpful to look for groups that complement you while perhaps using different tactics. If you want to take a "peaceful" route with a letter-writing campaign you might try to hook up with a direct action group who will do more aggressive protesting, as well as a legal group to threaten lawsuits tailored to your message.

Example: Dan can list a few potential allies easily, the other student groups devoted to the environment, and national groups promoting recycling (such as the Global Recycling Network or the National Recycling Coalition). A little additional thought offers other potential allies: the companies that do (and profit from) the recycling itself. Local community boards wanting to keep the city clean. Even something as off topic as homeless advocates who know some of the homeless help support themselves by collecting discarded recyclable products can produce people who will help with the march.

Goal: List every group you can think of that might support your cause and join you in protests. The Internet, local community centers, and universities are a good place to start looking. Once you have this list, ask them to suggest groups you may have missed.

The Media

The media are critical of almost any protest. Since your overall goal should be to shape public opinion, the media can be the best way to get your message out to the public. Know what media are likely to cover your protest. This includes such normal media as local television, newspapers, and radio, as well as less traditional media. Are there locally printed magazines that might cover you? Web sites devoted to your cause or your city? Student newspapers at local colleges? Public television shows you can get airtime on? Radio stations run out of local colleges?

The further in advance you start working with the media, the better. You want to cultivate your relationship with key reporters, learn what they want and need to put out good stories, and develop a reputation for giving it to them. This may be more relevant (and easier) for groups that plan to put on more than one protest over time, but even if you think you are only going to organize a single protest, your relationship with the media will be a key element of your success or failure.

Example: Dan lists the media who may cover a march to city hall: all the local and student newspapers, the campus radio and local radio stations, the local TV news, the weeklies, and so on. With the resources they have, they also decide to put up a Web site themselves, letting them be the media and control a little of how their message goes out. One of the club members agrees to collect contact information for members of the media and serve as media liaison.

Goal: List all media likely to cover your protest. If you have time, look at how they are likely to cover your protest, and set up at least one person as a full-time media liaison, responsible for giving information to the media and answering questions.

The Authorities/Police

Protests, by their nature, create conflict, and any time you create conflict in today's society the authorities tend to come down on you. However, even if things get ugly, you must understand that the police are not your enemy. Read that again, because it is important: *The police are not your enemy.* Even if they are going to arrest you, even if you are protesting something like police brutality or racism, you must realize that the line cops are just there to do a job. Some cops (like some of any group) may be racist, clueless, and acting illegally, but setting out to make the authorities your direct enemy diverts energy you will need elsewhere. The local government is probably not evil (sometimes large, bulky, and stupid, but not evil). If you can get these people to work with you, your overall goal (shaping public opinion and creating change) will be much easier.

That said, never allow the powers that be to dictate terms that will neutralize your work. If the only way you can get a permit to march is to go miles away from the public, you may just have to go without a blessing from on high. What a pity.

A little research here will also pay off. Take a look at where the authorities are physically. Know how many minutes it takes the cops to get from the nearest police station to your protest site. Look at who has jurisdiction over what areas (you can have all kinds of fun with city cops by being five feet outside the city limits). Look at the force response on protests in the past: Have the cops just sent a few officers to watch marches in the past or have they always arrived in riot gear? If they did it before, odds are they'll do it again.

Example: The student group has not yet decided if they plan to get a permit or march without one, but either way cops may take a march poorly. In addition, the city council itself, businesses along the march route (who may not like the disruption), the university itself (who may dislike having its name dragged into the argument), are all potential sources of conflict.

Goal: Know what authorities you will come in conflict with. List them, and list how each is likely to respond to your actions. If you have the time and the ability to do so, get permission for what you plan to do (permits for marches, rented space for speeches, and so on). If you are going to come into dramatic conflict, knowing that ahead of time will let you plan for it.

The Public

These are the people you are trying to influence. Every step of the way you must look at how your actions will impact the public. Never march just to march, never get up on a soapbox just to hear yourself talk. You may have a very specific audience (parents of children in public high school, people in an area with a growing homeless population) or a very broad one (everyone in a nation that has gone to war), but by knowing who you are talking to you can shape what you say appropriately.

Example: While the public may broadly support a concept like recycling, in times of short budgets people may want to cut recycling rather than cut other areas. The group decides that they need to not only communicate the pro-recycling message, but convince people that it must be a priority.

Goal: Identify whose opinion you want to change, how you want them to think, and what they think now. Keep this information in your mind every step of the way.

Your Target

Perhaps the most effort should be put into studying your target, what they are doing, how they operate, what they can do to fulfill your demands. The more you understand how they work the more ways you will find to disrupt their operations, and the better prepared you will be on the unlikely chance they simply come out and ask, "What do you want us to do?"

Look at what you can do to impact the "bottom line" of your target (such as revenue for corporations or votes for politicians). No matter what your target's opinions, when you impact their bottom line they will sit up and take notice.

If you have the time, research how your target has dealt with protesters in the past. If they flipped out before, odds are they'll flip out again.

Example: In this case the group wants to create change in the policy of the city government. These people rely on votes, and a call during the march to vote people out of office who don't protect the environment and quality/beauty of the city will strike a chord with the politicians. Understanding how policy gets created will let the group make a call to the specific committee responsible for the budget that can restore the recycling funding the group wants.

Goal: Know who your target is, and how you want them to act. Think about how they are likely to react. Insure that your target can really create the change you want.

What Has Come Before: Protests in History

The Cold War was a time of great national worry, with people doing everything from building bomb shelters to leaving the country. New York City began conducting citywide annual civil defense drills in 1955, designed to simulate the conditions of a nuclear war. During the drills everyone in the city was required to take shelter.

Ammon Hennacy and Dorothy Day, two members of the Catholic Workers Movement, led 28 others who refused to, as they put it, "play this silly war game." Over the years the drills were held, they were regularly arrested for noncompliance and held for 30 days at a time, but the attention they received brought others to their cause. By 1961 over 2,000 people joined them, risking arrest to protest the civil defense drills. In the face of this consistent opposition, the drills stopped the following year.

Chapter Four
The Importance of Having Clear Goals

Once people are confronted with the issues that get them fired up it is easy to want to take action, want to get into the streets, want to grab some friends and sit on a CEO's desk and demand change. But if you don't protest with a clear set of goals, if you don't know what you want the world to look like, you run the risk of not only being ineffective but of wasting the effort and energy of everyone working with you.

24

Clear, stated goals also answer the important question: When do we stop protesting? Protests are great vehicles for social change, but no one should want to have to go this route. Protests are a sign that the system has broken down, that people have been unable to find other ways to communicate and work together. By knowing what goals you are trying to achieve, once you achieve them you can go back to a more harmonious life (or on to the next issue to protest).

In order to be good goals for a protest, your goals must be both specific and measurable. Saying that you want to protect the environment is a good thought, but it is not a specific goal. Even saying that you want to protect local water quality is, while a good idea, not a specific goal. Wanting the Dow chemical plant to stop dumping chemical waste into the water to halt the death of local fish is a good, measurable, specific goal. You have to define what victory means, what indicates that you have achieved your aims.

With a goal like that you have a clear endpoint that you can communicate to the company, the media, and the public. It is easy for everyone involved to see what you want, even if they don't agree with you. You have a clear point at which you can stop your protests (at least the ones related to that issue). And you can show clear results. Has Dow stopped dumping chemicals? Has the local fish population recovered? A focus on clear measurable goals helps keep everyone on track and gives validity and a sense of purpose to everyone involved.

Ideally you should be able to state your goals in one short sentence. You want the public and the media to have a clear, immediate idea of why you are protesting and what you want to happen. If your goals are overly broad or overly complex you will have difficulty communicating the purpose behind your actions, and can be dismissed more easily by people unwilling to take the time to understand the situation. It is important to have the background and depth to be able to speak about the details of your issue, but if people never get the key ideas the details don't matter. Some issues (such as globalization) do not lend themselves to sound bites, but try to be as concise as you can.

One way to determine if your goals are workable is to imagine the (highly unlikely) situation in which your target gives in as soon as you show up and agrees to do anything you ask. If the CEO of Dow walks up to you and says, "OK, you win, what do you want me to do?," What do you tell him? Protect the environment? What does that mean? If you have clearly measurable, specific goals, goals someone can act on, you can tell him directly what you want done.

Goal: Ask yourself "What is my goal for this protest? What do I want to accomplish or change?" Write it down in several different ways. Is it specific? Measurable? Is the key idea easy to understand and explain?

Example: Continuing the above example, the student group looks at its goals. Just promoting recycling proves to be too broad a goal. Instead they want to pressure the city council to vote again on the issue of funding the recycling program, and return to the old funding level of $5,000 per fiscal quarter.

What Has Come Before: Protests in History

The South was a hotbed of protest during the Sixties as people of all colors fought for an integrated society and rights for people of color. But not all of the protests produced gains. In Albany, Georgia, in 1961-62 the Student Nonviolent Coordinating Committee and the Southern Christian Leadership Conference joined together to stage a series of nonviolent actions to protest segregation. They held marches, sit-ins, and boy-cotts, worked to raise awareness and public involvement, and were willing to risk arrest, economic cost, and personal harm to fight for what they believed in.

All this power and energy, however, came to little effect. By aiming too high and trying to do too much at once (trying to integrate all of society at once, instead of aiming at specific public places), and by failing to work as a unified force (in-fighting between the groups was common) the protests failed to produce the results people wanted, and had much less im-pact than many of the other, better run protests of the era. Their goals were too broad (integrate all of society), and in the end that dissipated their energy and effectiveness. A more fo-cused goal might have had more success.

Chapter Five
Protest Highlight: Marches

Marches have been a staple of protests for as long as people could walk. There are numerous advantages to marches, including mobility, high exposure, public recognition and support. People are comfortable with marches as a way to protest, so you can get your message to them in a way they are willing to deal with. Always keep in mind that you are marching to get a point across to the public. Do not march just to march. Do not march to make yourself feel better. Do not march because you don't know what else to do. March to communicate your point.

As a classic method of protest, a march may be your best tool for getting your message across to the public. Let's look at a timeline for a march. Here's what you need to do, and when.

Before the March

Plan your route: Marches are mobile protests, and the most critical issue for a march is where you go.

Start points: You need a clear starting point with a gathering area large enough to support everyone you'll have coming. Ideally, try to get space that will support 20% more than the maximum number of people you think will show up, just in case. Good start points include parks, large parking lots, and college campuses.

You also want to select areas that have good visibility, somewhere you can set up signs, chant and get passers-by interested. Look for areas with lots of open space and easy access. For that reason, bad areas include inside buildings or other enclosed areas that people cannot easily get to, or that could be easily cut off by authorities.

March route: There are three key elements that affect the ideal route for your march. These are visibility, distance, and interference. Your goal is to get your message to the public, so a route down major streets and in front of large buildings, especially media offices, works well. As for distance, this is a march, not a hike. You don't want to wear out your marchers, so it should probably not take more than a few hours, at a very slow walk, to go from your start to your end points. If you have time, walk your route ahead of time to pace it out.

Remember that if the people at the front of the march move too quickly you risk having the back end get slightly separated and allowing the cops to more easily cut you off. Finally, you want to look at how your route might be affected by people who want to stop your protest. Going over a major bridge? Near a police station? Plan alternate routes, and make sure all your people have maps, just in case.

Your route may be heavily impacted if you are getting permits for your march, as you will have to put up with the restrictions of the city issuing the permits. As long as you stay visible and can get your message across this is fine, and the additional support you can get will help. If the city or issuing authority will only give you a permit to march on a back road or out of the way area you have to consider marching without a permit.

Plan a few alternate routes in case you get cut off. Look at the section on how you will be fucked with for more details.

End point: The first issue about the end point of your march: have one. Marches with no clear place to go have no choice but to run into problems as the march goes on and winds down, and the confusion will hurt your message. The same points that help you select a start point work here, and you should plan to support 20-40% more people than you had at the start to support the people you pick up as you go. If you plan to just break up when you hit your end point you can get by with a smaller space, and an interior area may work for you, but you should plan on at least some people sticking around for a while.

End points are usually selected based on your target or goals, and who you want to hear your message. Places like the mayor's office or a corporate headquarters are always possible, as are media offices, but anywhere that your target will get your message is acceptable.

30

March variant: the snake march. In some cases (such as when the authorities want to simply shut down marches as soon as they start) a "point A to point B" march may not be an option. One way to get around police barricades is to set up a snake march, a march with a clear start point and several, unannounced, possible targets in mind. For example a march might head into downtown wanting to arrive at the federal building, get deflected by a line of cops, redirect to head to the mayor's office (forcing the cops to run all over to create new barricades), get deflected again and wind up outside of the offices of the city council. By having a handful of possible targets, all of which will work for your protest, you can make it next to impossible for the cops to shut you down. This can be much harder to set up and maintain than a traditional march, and maps and strong communications are a must, but in areas with very aggressive cops this may be the only option.

Pre-march communications: Media contacts. As far in advance as possible compile a list of the media you want to alert to your march. Get contact names, numbers, and e-mail addresses, for as many media members as you can in the time you have. Take a look at the chapter on how to deal effectively with the media for details on what to tell the press.

Other organizations: Try to include as many other organizations as you can as early as possible. If they know what your schedule is they can plan to assist more fully, and you can divide the labor more evenly. Remember, if you burn out before the march even starts, you're not doing anyone any good.

Community centers, campuses, and public gathering points: Put up flyers or posters in as many places in your community as you can think of, listing why you are marching, when, and the start and end points of your march. If you can put these up a few weeks before you march, and keep them up until you start, you will get a better turnout.

The authorities: If you are going to get permits and permission to march, do so as far in advance as possible. If you leave it to the last minute anyone who wants to shut you down can do so simply by delaying your permit review or paperwork. Find out how much time they require to review your requests, and meet whatever deadlines they have. If you look unprofessional by missing deadlines, why should they think you have it together enough to hold a march? Also realize that even if you do get permission and permits ahead of time the powers that be may try to change your requirements at the last minute. This may prevent you from getting the permits for the routes or actions you want to take. Expect this, and expect that even if you try to get permits you may have to go without them.

Also realize that even if you don't plan to alert the authorities to what you are doing and you plan to march without asking anyone for permission, as soon as you alert the public to what you are doing you alert the authorities. This is largely unavoidable, so don't go in assuming you can pull the wool over the eyes of everyone all the time.

Props: Ah, where would we be without toys? While in theory you can march with nothing more than a loud voice and a good pair of shoes, you'll do much better with a bit of support material. The specifics of what you need will be determined by the subject of your protest, but a few basics are constant: signs, water, and appropriate clothing.

Take a look at the chapter on protest survival packs for more information on what to bring if you have time to pack.

During the March

If you plan ahead well, and if no one gives you too much trouble (good luck), the march itself should be the easiest part of the whole process. There are a few key steps to the march itself.

Timing: Try to start your march on time, but expect last minute delays to slow you down. Planning to start out at 6:30 and not getting going before 6:40 is fine. Not getting started until 8:00 is unacceptable. Most marches don't get going until at least half an hour past the listed start time, but barring someone lying dead in the street you need to start no later than an hour after your posted start time. People joining your march and other friendly groups will be expecting you to adhere to these times, and leaving very late makes you look unprofessional and hurts your ability to shape public opinion.

Movement: This is a march, not a stand, so you need to get moving and stay moving. If you have the personnel, devote a few people exclusively to keeping the marchers moving at close to the same speed. If large groups of people slow down it will drag your march down. On the other hand, this isn't a race, and you want to move slow enough to get your message across and pick up additional marchers. Overall, speed isn't your biggest issue, just make sure you stay moving. Watch to make sure you stay more or less together, and avoid spreading out far enough that the police can cut you off and break you into small, easily managed groups. When in doubt, slow down, and your communications people should be sure to remind those in the front of the march to slow down when necessary.

Motivation: Always keep in mind that the participants in your march are there voluntarily and will have vastly different tolerances for march style, participation, and risk. While things are going well you need to encourage the more flamboyant to chant, keep the signs held high, and so on, and make sure everyone knows where to go. If things start to get tense, you need to keep your people calm and as rational as possible. When the air is full of tear gas it is very hard to keep order, but at the very least you have a responsibility to keep your focus. There is more on contingency plans later in this chapter.

Support: Marches depend on several key factors to run smoothly. By making sure you have a few key support elements planned before the march you can concentrate on your message during the march.

Communications: Marches are dynamic events. You are trying to move hundreds of people, keep your message loud and vibrant, and avoid problems ranging from distracted protesters to police tear gas. Keeping your lines of communication with your fellow protest organizers is critical. The size of your march determines the communications options available to you, but most of the time you should look at combining electronic and non-electronic communications. Each protest organizer should have either a cell phone or a walkie-talkie (available at Radio Shack). Also, if you have the manpower you should have two or three people with a lot of stamina to constantly walk up and down the length of the march checking in with the protest organizers and relaying information, such as police activity, reroutes, and so on. And, of course, once the tear gas hits, bullhorns may be your only option.

In addition, most protests blend chants and songs promoting your cause into the march, both to communicate your message, keep morale high and promote a sense of solidarity among the marchers.

Your runners doing communication also double well as your Peacekeepers.

Peacekeepers: You need to provide your own eyes and ears as security during your march. This may not be a major concern in small marches, but be looking out for at least the following situations/people:

Infiltrators: One tactic that has become increasingly popular is to find a protest that you disagree with and go "join" it, to go over the top and make them look foolish. Nike did this quite effectively by hiring "protesters" to use the tactics that legitimate protests had used in the past to "protest" the new Nike shoes, claming they were too good, too effective, and gave too great an advantage to the team that wore them. This had the effect of simultaneously getting Nike publicity for their new shoes and damaging the true protest by deflecting attention away from the real issues regarding Nike.

During your march you should look for people taking your core message to extremes and trying to make *that* the message that gets to the media, thus hurting your credibility. An example: If you are running a pro-choice march, look for the people with the signs and photos arguing that women should be allowed to abort all the way up to right before birth, perhaps with signs like "Kill the unborn, not our rights."

If you have to deal with people like this, the best response may be to surround them with people speaking your true message and try to drown them out. At the very least you have to marginalize these people. For the more aggressive, if you plan ahead you can build protest signs specifically designed to spear and take down signs you want to keep off camera. A sharp point and a good thrust can be more effective than hours of talking (just make sure you spear the sign and not the person holding it). Take a look at the chapter on advanced protest tactics for more information on what to look for.

Sanitation: If your march is going to go on for a long time or over a long distance you and your protest organizers, as well as the marchers, will need a pit stop from time to time. For the most part people will find ways to take care of their needs, but if you have permits and permission for your march you may be able to arrange with the city to provide sanitation facilities. If not, look at your march route and try to find businesses or facilities along the way that may be sympathetic to your cause, and speak with the owner about allowing you and your march organizers to pop in for a pit stop on your way by. Ideally none of your marchers will need to stop ("You should have gone before we left the house"), but having a few places along the way will help keep you focused.

Media relations: Your goal in a march is to shape public opinion, and part of that is getting your face in front of the cameras. If your march is any good at all you will attract media, newspaper reporters, television cameras. How these media cover your work will have a major impact on how effective all your work is. You should have at least one person whose sole job during the march is to communicate with the media, and especially to anyone with a camera, to ensure they know exactly why you are marching and what your goals are. This person needs to be able to speak confidently, state your goals in one clear sentence, look good on camera, and stay cool if things go badly. They should also give reporters cards with contact names and numbers for follow-up information, and get reporters' names to contact them after the march. You always want reporters getting information and facts from your perspective.

Entertainment: With a few exceptions (such as funeral processions) marches are and should be fun, festive events. People dress up in weird costumes, chant, sing songs and play drums. This is important for attracting passers-by into the march, keeping morale up, and helping to bond marchers together as a group. Ask your friends to dress up, call in some musicians, and make an event of it. The issues you are fighting for may be deadly serious, but you don't always need to be.

Non-protest support personnel: There are two main groups that are not related to your march, but that you need to have ready and work with if you are going to march (or perform any protest) to maximum effect. As far ahead of time as possible try to arrange for a team of legal observers to join your march. These are non-participants, frequently law students, who act as an impartial set of eyes and ears in case anything occurs that lands you in jail or court. On the witness stand both you and the police have clear agendas, but legal observers (in theory anyway) do not. Even if you think everything will go smoothly, try to arrange for a few legal observers, but if things are likely to go badly legal observers are a must.

On the subject of things going badly, the second group of people to have lined up are lawyers, the people who will work with your people as they get arrested, to get you back on the street. Again, even if you think things will go well, have a few lawyers on standby, and if you expect police involvement lawyers are a must. Your local phone book will list dozens if not hundreds of lawyers, but legwork is critical here. Ask about their experience with protests, their fees, and shop around. After you get their prices, tell them what you are protesting. Many times you can find lawyers who will offer a discount or work for free. In some cases you can also simply rely on public defenders to handle some cases, but you owe it to the people who may be getting arrested next to you to have good support set up ahead of time.

After the March

Once you reach your end point and the march is over, assuming you're all still out of jail and more or less together, you have a final opportunity to get your message across. If you've selected your end point well, you might want to rally together to make a few speeches, distribute information about ways marchers can continue to help your cause, pass the hat to collect a few bucks (in addition to having passed the hat at the start), and let people disperse peacefully. If that's what you're going to do make sure you do the following:

Make sure the media has what it needs. Give anybody with a camera a card with your group's media contact, a way to contact you, and the core message you're trying to get across. Offer to make a statement on camera, and make sure your speeches are held in a way that lets the cameras get a good shot. You may want to bring flashlights so you can light your speakers, and find an elevated point so they are above the crowd. Take note of what media is there. Get contact information for any reporter who will give it to you, especially print reporters, so you can contact them later to follow up and make sure they have everything they need to cover you in the best light you can get.

Gather public information. Marches are a great way to network with people who agree with your cause, so you can take this opportunity to set up signup sheets and get people's names, numbers and e-mail addresses. Not everyone will want to sign up, but every voice you add to your cause helps.

Now, at the end of the march you may not be just making a few speeches and walking off into the night. You may want to turn the march into a different form of protest, from a sit-in to a blockade. Once you have a few hundred people rallied ready to protest in support of the homeless, you may want to camp out on the governor's lawn to make your speeches. Marches transition quite well into other forms of protests, so take a look at the appropriate chapter and get ready to give the governor a piece of your mind.

Bring a toothbrush.

How You Will Be Fucked With

Here's the really interesting part. If you need to protest something, odds are there will be people who want to shut you up, shut you down, and shut you out. Expect that at every step of the way people are going to be working to either stop your march entirely or reduce its effectiveness. If you know ahead of time how people are going to fight you, you can be much more effective. Here are some ways marches get stopped:

Permit Denial/rerouting/last minute demands: City and federal governments tend not to like marches and protests, and so may try to find reasons to deny you a permit to march. Laws and regulations vary from city to city, but popular objections include the noise, the crowds, and the disruption marches will cause. If you run into problems getting permits, expect to need a lawyer, and be prepared to sue to get the permits you require (or simply go without permits).

The more subtle way to marginalize a march is to insist it be rerouted, usually through a much less populated area. You may be offered a permit, but not on a main street or not through downtown. If the proposed area works for you, having a permit is better than not having a permit, but if it prevents you from doing justice to your message then hold out for the route you need. In the end, you always have the option of marching without a permit, and you may be able to use that fact as leverage when negotiating with the paper pushers.

Governments may also tack on demands and requirements at the last minute in the interest of shutting you down. One popular requirement is that you carry insurance for your event, often to the tune of a million dollars or more. Usually, last minute demands indicate that the powers that be don't want you to act at all, and signal that you may have to act without permission from on high.

Separation: This is a popular police tactic for dealing with large marches. The cops allow the march to go a certain distance, and then bring in a wall of cops to cut the march into smaller groups. If they can reroute large groups of your people your march becomes much easier for them to manage. You can counter this in a few ways: Your runners should be watching side streets for masses of cops (who will usually try to cut you off at intersections), and you should try to keep people moving at more or less the same rate. If you keep people from getting too far ahead or behind and stay in one mass of people you become very hard to separate.

In addition, if you've planned backup routes to your final destination and your march gets separated then your protest organizers in each group may be able to simply take different routes to get to the same endpoint.

Tear gas/chemical disruption: Ah, the old standby of cops everywhere. Tear gas is used by police for two key reasons: It disperses people from the area of effect and it discourages people from moving into that area. Tear gas canisters (as well as "stun" grenades, bean bag shotguns, and the like) are used when the cops have decided you have gotten out of hand.

Tear gas is also used because it tends to work. It is remarkably hard to keep marching when you can't see or breathe. As part of the gear you carry you may want to include a bandana, rag or cloth (soaked in vinegar or lime juice to counter the chemicals) that you can hold over your mouth and nose, and this will somewhat mitigate the effects. If you have the desire and resources you can also try carrying full gas masks (or industrial respirators and goggles), which work much better, but have two downsides. First, they make it hard to shout out your slogans and communicate with your fellow marchers, and second if the cops see a large number of marchers with gas masks they tend to take that badly and escalate much more rapidly. This may not be a bad thing, but know what you are getting into, and keep the masks hidden until needed.

Communication disruption: A disorganized protest is much easier for the cops to control or shut down. In addition to trying to separate you, they may choose to try to cut your lines of communication. Radios and cell phones may make running your march much easier to control, but devices exist to block cell phones, and cops are acquiring and using these (even though doing so is illegal) if it will help shut protesters up.

Cops or other authorities may also disrupt communications by tearing down signs, or even ripping them from people's hands. All you can do in response is to have so many signs, or backups, that they cannot get them all, and to try to make sure their actions are in the eyes of the media. Forcing your target to show their frustration works in your interest.

In addition, carrying a bullhorn makes you a great target for harassment or arrest. You can deal with this by making sure your runners are keeping everyone informed, and not relying on any one way of communicating. Having a few protest organizers on bikes to move up and down the line helps, and in a pinch you can use call and response, yelling something that gets repeated down the line until it reaches the people who need to hear it. Keep the phones on. Keep the bullhorns loud. Keep your runners talking. And your march keeps going.

Weather: Mother Nature is not partial to who she rains or snows on. The truly pissed off will march and yell and scream in any weather, but a hard rain will do more than anything the cops can do to cut your numbers.

There may not be much you can do about the weather, but prepare for it. If you anticipate rain, waterproof your signs. If you are marching through Phoenix in July, don't wear costumes that cover you in latex and faux fur. Forgetting the weather is an easy mistake, but it happens all the time.

Dissent from within/Stupid people with bricks: Any time you get masses of people together and get them riled up there will be some people who just want to rage and cause trouble. These people can do more damage to you than anything else because they make it easy to dismiss you as violent anti-social loons, and they tend to make good photo ops for the evening news.

Everyone you have coordinating your march should be watching for people out to cause trouble, but your peacekeepers should be the first to deal with these people. Most of the time you can talk them back into line and keep the march going calmly. If they are really gone you may have to put yourself between the brick and the window and try to talk them back into line. Either way, try to keep it off the evening news and keep the cameras busy with something else.

Arrest: The last resort of the police, mass arrest sometimes becomes the weapon of choice. Once you have been protesting for a while you can watch the cops and see when they go from observers to participants, and when and where they are planning to move in and arrest people. This will usually occur after your march has been stopped, and may or may not come with much warning. Definitely take a look at the chapter on the police and your rights, and if you get to this stage there are a few points to keep in mind:

- *Never run from the police.* Police will react much more violently if you run. If your march is prevented from moving, your best option is to sit down wherever you are and perhaps link hands.
- *Never resist arrest or fight the police.* You don't need to cooperate with the cops, but fighting the cops serves as the perfect excuse for them to get really rough with you, and it is better to end up in jail than the hospital.
- *Stay on camera.* If you are going to get arrested, do everything you can to get arrested in front of the media. Arrests make great news, and this can serve as a wonderful way to let the public know that your cause is out there and that people care enough about it to go to jail.

Overall, marches are a classic protest method, and they may serve you as the best way to get your message across. Get your group together, get a good pair of shoes, and get out in the streets.

March Checklist:

Personnel:
- ☐ Media liaison
- ☐ Police liaison
- ☐ Lawyer(s)
- ☐ Legal observers
- ☐ Peacekeepers/security
- ☐ Medical personnel
- ☐ Runners

Toys:

- ☐ Banners
- ☐ Signs
- ☐ Tape/spray paint
- ☐ Maps
- ☐ Food/drink
- ☐ Still/video cameras

What Has Come Before:
Protests in History

One way to ensure protests have impact is to think big. Scale can add weight to any protest, as was demonstrated in 1960 by the Committee for Nonviolent Action. Some marches run across a city, or across a state, but the CNVA held a nine-month, 6,000-mile march across the United States, through Europe and to Moscow, holding rallies to protest atomic testing along the way. People on all sides of the debate tended to blame the "other side" and other governments for the nuclear situation, but by targeting both superpowers and being evenhanded and willing to tell all sides how they felt the CNVA gained credibility that other, smaller protests of the day lacked.

Chapter Six
Protest Highlight: Pickets

Picket lines have long been a classic means of getting your message directly in front of the people most able to do something to help you. Why picket? Picket lines have several advantages as a form of protest. Picket lines require less logistical and support work than many other forms of protest, can be set up and run with very little advance notice, and have direct impact on the people you are trying to influence. Every day a plant manager has to walk past a picket line of workers he has no choice but to think about why those workers are there. Keeping signs and picketers in front of abortion and family planning clinics will force everyone going to them to think hard about why they are there, and may discourage some from going at all.

Pickets also have the advantage of being a relatively safe form of protest. You don't have the logistical problems of moving large numbers of people, as in a march, and picket lines tend to be less confrontational than blockades or sit-ins. You get to make your point, and you (maybe) get to stay out of jail.

This chapter assumes that you may, for example, be picketing the mayor's press conference but that you won't be trying to stop him from being able to get to the conference. If you want to stop the mayor you're a blockade, not a picket line, and that has very much its own rules. See the blockade chapter for more details.

So how do you go about running an effective picket? Here are the steps of a successful picket line.

Before the Picket Line

Picket lines can be run with less planning and can be set up in less time than other large-scale protests, but a little planning goes a long way. Picket lines require a lot of people, and step one is to get as many people as possible to join the line. If you are workers going on strike, your manpower can be pulled from the company directory, but if you're picketing a political convention or a corporate headquarters, you have to set up a large support pool as far in advance as you can.

One major problem with the logistics of a picket line is the large number of people who need to be informed of what's going on. Before the picket line gets going, try to recruit as many assistants as you can to serve as team organizers, people who will march in shifts to lead chants, make sure signs are held high, and keep morale up. For a quick picket that only needs to last as long as the mayor is speaking you may be able to do everything yourself, but a strike lasting weeks requires a much larger support network. As a rule of thumb, try to have one team organizer for every 20 line protesters, and plan to change out team organizers every four to six hours to avoid burning out. People on the line should be asked how long they want to stay, but probably should not be on the line more than four hours at a stretch. Really pumped up and dedicated people may want to keep going longer but remember that if you are picketing for the long term, burnout becomes a factor.

Communications with your own people should also be planned as far in advance as possible. For long-term picket lines each team organizer should have the phone number (and cell, if possible) for every other team organizer. In many cases you will want to use code names for your protest organizers and some simple code to disguise the cell numbers (such as adding one to each number, so 728-7574 becomes 839-8685) in order to prevent the cops from arresting one person, seizing the cards, and thus finding all the rest of the people they want to arrest. Three-by-five cards with these numbers should be standard equipment. Since the picket line won't be moving too far, you can function without a complicated communications plan, but at the very least someone on the line should always have a cell phone in case situations change or they need to call in relief or backup.

In addition, as with all protests, you need to plan for dealing with the media. Your goal may not be to influence the public at large, for example, a picket line coupled with a strike where you want to affect contract negotiations, but it never hurts to

48

get good coverage on the eleven o'clock news. Have the contact numbers for your local media, especially the television stations, and have a public relations statement ready to go. Whenever anything of note occurs "on the line" make sure the media knows. From notifying them that you've started your protest to letting them know the first time the cops show up, keep calling and e-mailing the media as often as you can. Don't worry about bothering them, or overwhelming them with detail. Just stay in front of them.

You don't necessarily need to alert the media, or anyone else, ahead of time that you will be protesting. If you alert them you may also alert your target, who can then change plans to get around you. In addition there are many circumstances, such as political speeches, where you can rely on the media being there anyway.

The last thing you need to do before the picket can be its best is to gather as much information about your target as you can. If you want to get your signs in front of the mayor at a dinner you need to know when and how he or she will arrive. Gathering information about your target can be very difficult, and will be different for every protest. It is beyond the scope of this work to cover every piece of intelligence you can gather, but suffice it to say that the more research you can do the more effective your protest will be.

During the Protest

If things go well, the only things you have to do during the protest are the things you planned to do when you set it up.

The key point of a picket line is to communicate your dissatisfaction to someone (the mayor, the school board, and so on). In order to do that effectively you have to communicate to three groups: the target, the media, and the public. Here are some tips and tricks for getting your message across.

You communicate your message to your target the old-fashioned way, by yelling it at them. The single most important thing you will decide when you plan your picket line is where to line up. In some cases it may seem obvious, but look at who will see you and when. Ask yourself: Who am I trying to talk to? Where will they be?

Protesting a company's hiring practices? You may initially think of walking in front of the company's main lobby (in front of that nice photogenic company logo). But if all the upper management enter the building through a back parking lot, do you want to line up there instead? Or can you rally the personnel to do both? Remember that you're not trying to stop anyone from moving around, you just want to get your message in their face and keep it there.

If you are in your target's face, but not visible to anyone else, you can be safely ignored. You communicate with the media and the public as a means to influencing your target. A company may want to hide prejudicial hiring practices, but once the media digs into them it becomes very hard to keep things hidden. Schools may not want to fund a band or a drama group, but when your picket line gets a few hundred parents screaming at them the money may be found pretty quickly.

The best way to get attention to your cause is to ensure that the media has all the information you can provide to support your cause. As soon as you set up your picket line you need to send faxes, send e-mails, and make phone calls to the local television stations, radio stations, newspapers and community centers making your case and providing information. One problem you can run into with the media is attention span. A new picket line is news; a line that's been chanting the same thing for a week may get bumped for something more dynamic. If you plan to have your line up for the long term you should plan on staging specific events during the picket to make news and keep your issue in the public light. Adding a rally to a picket line, getting a local celebrity to speak, or adding a particularly elaborate and striking visual display that will look good on TV may help keep eyeballs on you, and attention to your cause.

Have one person whose sole job is to act as a phone contact for your picketers. This is the person who makes sure everyone knows when to be on the line, and is the first point of contact for your people.

Have a schedule for who is walking the picket line when, and try to stick to your schedule for rotating walkers in and out. Many of your people, especially initially, may want to walk till they drop. This is a great attitude, but if all of your people burn out in the first day your line gets weak in later days. Let everyone know they can help best by being consistent for the long haul. Always reinforce the idea that you hope not to be there long, but that you need to plan as if you will be.

Make sure you keep morale up, keep people focused on why they are there. Every day that your protest goes on you are going to lose people. The more focused your people are on why they are there, the fewer you will lose. Try to have at least three reasons why you are there, and two different ways to show your people (or anyone else) why you are there. Picketing a biomedical facility? The photographic work you can show should keep your people pissed off. Protesting for higher pay? Bring a paycheck to show your people when emotions flag. People can argue with ideas and theories and people all they like, but the number on the check is the number on the check.

You also need to have visuals to support the picketers, signage and displays to communicate your point quickly and effectively to passers-by and the media. Take a look at the chapter on how to make a good sign, and remember to plan for the weather. Unlike for a march or other quick protest, the signs you are constructing may need to stand up for a long time. For other protests you might be able to get away with some cardboard and a marker, but for a picket line you may want to invest in some flat boards (easily acquired at your local hardware store) and a good dark paint. The two things to remember for these durable signs are: It needs to be light enough that people will not tire carrying it (so get a light-weight wood), and it needs to display your message well (so look for a light-colored wood and a dark paint). As your picket line will probably stay in one place you can also use larger, fixed signs that you can set up and leave in place. This lets you get your message across in a big way without having to haul wood around all day.

If you use pictures on your signs (which can be very, very effective) you can go beyond just taping them down by taking your signs to a local Kinko's and laminating them down. This way they will hold up much better under rain, wind, or hurled eggs.

For a long protest, sanitation becomes a major issue. As a gesture of goodwill your target may actually make services available (an employer during contract negotiations can usually be talked into this as they get a few brownie points and don't really have to do anything). Local restaurants or bars may also provide facilities in small quantities (talk to the management and play up how much business all those protesters will be bringing them). Failing any of this you may need to ask the city to supply porta-potties, but any way you do it you must have a sanitation facility that lets your people take care of their needs while staying off the line for the minimum time possible.

Unlike short-term protests such as marches or rallies, long-term protests such as picket lines introduce the need to concern yourself with food and drink for your protesters. You should encourage your people to pack a lunch and have someone who is responsible for making sure everyone's water bottles are filled regularly. Any picket line is tiring, and if you have to yell and carry on in the sun it is critical that everyone stay hydrated.

Many of the people who support your picket line, but do not want to (or cannot) be directly involved in creating conflict may be able to help by supplying food and drink. Especially for picket lines related to a strike the families of the strikers can get together, have lunch-making parties, and feel involved while supporting the picketers on the line.

A great morale booster can be to call in pizza, chicken, or other takeout for the line. You may be able to get food donations or discounts from local takeout joints in exchange for them being able to post signs plugging their support ("We support higher pay for local teachers" or "we support local union 387"). This is more likely to work if you have wide community support for your cause, and less likely to work for more heated, controversial issues, but it is worth looking into. *Tip:* If you're planning your protest in advance you may want to print up small signs that you can give to stores for just this purpose.

How You Will Be Fucked With

Picket lines are a well-established way of protesting, and there are quite a few established ways to fuck them up, with new ways coming up every protest. Here are a few of the things you should be looking out for.

Arrest: Any sufficiently obnoxious protest will draw the cops at some point, probably sooner rather than later. Prepare your people for this ahead of time by letting them know the cops may show up, and making sure everyone knows who is to deal with them when they show up.

Your big concern with the police is to ensure that you are not violating any more laws than you have to. If you walk into the street to make sure cars see your signs you may be arrested for obstructing traffic. It may be illegal to have a PA system without a permit. They may well want to harass you one way or another, but you can limit their options by knowing your local laws.

If/when the cops show up it is important to keep your people calm, and keep the protest going. DO NOT stop chanting, or holding your signs, or whatever just because the cops are there. You should have one person (or a small team) who will speak to the cops, answer questions, and let the rest of the picketers carry on with the protest. If the cops want to pull people out of the line, they will do so, if they want to arrest people they will do so, but always stay focused on the protest itself.

Tip: If the media, especially the television stations, are not already there when the cops show up, and especially if the cops show up in force, you should IMMEDIATELY call every local TV station you can and let them know what's going on. Having a camera pointed at them can do wonders for keeping the cops calm, and if you are going to get arrested it is far better to do it on live TV where the whole city can see how much you care for your cause.

Local laws: Pickets are a very well-known, traditional way to protest, and so most areas will have laws that relate directly to pickets (and are usually intended to make them harder to put on and run). These are going to vary from place to place, and you may not have to deal with any at all, but you have to do your homework ahead of time to ensure the cops can't trip you up and shut you down on some technicality.

Goading to violence: This may well be your biggest worry for protests that divide the community or inspire deep personal involvement. Any time you get people worked up, yelling and screaming, it is possible for someone to go a bit overboard. Someone who wants to shut down your protest can do so effectively by goading your people to violence. A cop quietly spewing racial slurs at black marchers can make the hottest protesters boil over. It is critical you keep your people calm enough to deal with this. If you throw the first punch your effectiveness for your cause is over, more so if you do so in front of news cameras. Violence may wind up being an element of any protest, but you don't want to be the one to bring it to that point. You protect yourself from this kind of goading by making sure your people hear a voice keeping them focused for every voice they hear trying to push them over the edge. Keep reminding them of why they are there, and above all, stay calm yourself. If the protest organizers lose it, the rank and file picketers are in bad shape.

Weather: Nature takes no sides, and your visibility can go down if the weather goes bad. There is not much you can do about the weather itself, but you can know what you may have to picket in.

Overall, picket lines are a lot of work, require a lot of people, and can require a lot of time, but they are a valuable tool for anyone who needs to increase awareness of a problem, and they have a track record of creating change. If you go to the picket line, and you go prepared, you will get results.

Picket Checklist:

Personnel:

☐ Media liaison
☐ Police liaison
☐ Company liaison
☐ Lawyer(s)
☐ Peacekeepers/security
☐ Medical personnel

Toys:

☐ Banners
☐ Signs
☐ Contact cards/phone tree
☐ Food/drink
☐ Still/video cameras

What Has Come Before: Protests in History

Well-organized picket lines and mass demonstrations can accomplish wonders, and in hindsight can create change that in later days looks truly amazing. In early 1943, Berlin saw the only organized protest of the Nazi Party's treatment of Jews to occur within Germany itself. During World War Two, the German government detained in Berlin thousands of German Jews. German Non-Jews, mostly women married to Jews who had been arrested, occupied a square adjacent to the detention center and picketed to demand their return, holding signs and chanting. At the peak the protesters were over six hundred strong, with thousands more filtering in and out, and they stayed in place even when the Gestapo ordered them to move and threatened to shoot anyone who stayed.

Joseph Goebbels, the Nazi Party authority for Greater Berlin, ordered about 1,700 Jews released. It is impossible to be sure what would have happened to these Jews had the protests failed, but the women in the square in that protest may very well have saved the lives of every one of the Jews released by the Nazis.

Chapter Seven
Protest Highlight: Blockades

Like picket lines and sit-ins, blockades make a point by bringing the problem directly into the face of the people involved. However, unlike more passive protests, blockades work to directly halt the offending parties and disrupt their activities in a more aggressive fashion. If you are standing in front of a board meeting holding signs so that board members must think of your issue when they get into their meeting you are a picket line. If you get a few of your closest friends and go block all the doors so the meeting cannot take place, you are a blockade.

This is clearly a much more aggressive method of protest, and should only be looked at if other avenues have been exhausted. You should be fully aware of the risks involved before you go this route. That said, when done correctly, blockades can be more effective in disrupting your target than more passive protests. Had the WTO in Seattle been surrounded only by picket lines the conference would have gone on more or less unhindered. The protesters willing to blockade the conference were a key element in bringing the conference to a halt.

Here are some things to think of when planning a blockade.

Before the Blockade

More than most protests, a blockade lives or dies on the planning and preparation done to set it up. A picket line can be a bit disorganized and get its point across, a march can be a bit unwieldy and still make the nightly news, but if a blockade isn't planned and executed correctly it will fall apart and be worse than useless.

The first step in planning a blockade is to do your homework. Research your target and where and when they will be operating. Trying to stop a board meeting? Get a map of the building they will be meeting in and map out the access points you need to block. It does you no good to seal the front door tight as a vault if they can just slip in a side loading dock. Trying to stop a logging team? You need a map of the access roads bulldozers will use. Every blockade will be different, but if you blow this step the rest falls apart.

A little legwork will pay off at this step, but you have to be careful. You may want to go physically look at the building involved to see for yourself what you need to block, but you don't want to be seen as casing the place. If the people of a logging firm have a meeting coming up and see a guy with scruffy hair and an "Earth First!" T-shirt jotting down notes, they are going to get a bit worried. Try to stay low key.

If you have the acting skills and risk tolerance for this sort of thing a little social engineering can go a long way here. Dress up and go claiming you are delivering donuts. Drive by and deliver the morning paper. Show up looking for a job interview. If people think you are just confused or lost they can be quite informative. This may well place you into very gray legal areas, but if you are planning a blockade you're probably going over that line anyway. It is critical that you have an honest assessment of your appearance and demeanor in order to know how you will be viewed as you do your recon. Just putting your long scruffy hair up in a ponytail does not make you look like a job applicant. Whoever does your recon may have to cut their hair, shave, and dress the part. One good check is to ask someone you don't know what you do for a living, based on how you appear. If they say anything far left, try again.

Once you have a good idea of the terrain you'll be working in, you can determine how many people you need for your blockade to work. If you just want to block the main doors for the symbolism (and media coverage) you may only need a few people. If you need to block all the access ways, you need quite a few more. You also need to include people as backups, and a few people to provide mobile support and communications (it is nice to have a pair of eyes that can walk around the block to see if the cops are massing). The number you will need will be different for every blockade, but plan on at least 10-15% extra for backup and to cover for anyone who can't show up at the last minute.

Over the line: One important issue with blockades is the restrictions you place on people's freedom of movement. If you blockade all the doors of a building to keep people out you are breaking laws, but if you block all the doors while people are inside you may be guilty of kidnapping.

With your map and personnel lined up you can plan your timeline. The duration of your blockade will be determined primarily by your target. If you want to shut down a conference you may only need to be in place for a day or a weekend. If you are trying to halt loggers you may be in the trees for a good long time.

Your timeline needs to include the following:

- When you move into position. More than anything else, it is critical that you block all access points and be in position at the same time. Another concern is how early you need to be in place in order to block the movement of the people you want to stop.

- How long you plan to be in position. If you know you can be in position for just a few hours to accomplish your goal, make sure everyone knows when they can go home.

- Any other preset events. It may be hard to plan ahead (that's what your backup people are for) but if you have any preset actions or know of any preset actions from your target (such as the time the mayor is scheduled to show up), make sure those times are listed.

As a quick legal note, you may find it in your best interest not to write any of this down, as anything you have written down may find its way into court. If you keep it simple your people should be able to remember the key points.

You also need to look at what equipment you need to maintain the blockade. This is going to be largely determined by the location and duration of the protest, but certain things are standard. The most important item for a blockade is U-locks, lock boxes or other devices to lock your protesters in place and prevent the cops from moving you easily. You also want to have at least one walkie-talkie or cell phone at each access point to stay in contact with each other. If you can, try to have a still or video camera to record what happens in case your target or the police get overly aggressive (but again remember that anything recorded can turn up in court, so keep that in mind). For multi-day protests you need food and water for each of your people. (Your extra people can try to bring in food, but they can be easily cut off and pizza drivers usually won't deliver across police lines.)

Other equipment will be determined by your specific event needs. Going to be protesting through the night? Gonna need flashlights. Standing out in the cold and rain? Bring jackets. A few moments spent ahead of time will save you a great deal of grief during your protest.

One final issue you must go over before doing something as confrontational as a blockade is the risk assessment of each of the people involved. The risk of violence and incarceration is much higher with a blockade than with other protests, and you and your people need to be fully committed to what you are doing. Read the section on risk assessment, and talk to everyone involved ahead of time.

During the Blockade

Once the blockade gets rolling, things will be moving fast and it can be easy to lose track of what you are doing and what needs to be done. Planning out what you want to happen, and looking at contingency plans, can help ensure your blockade serves its purpose. Here are some of the things to think of for the time of the blockade itself.

Communications: If you only need to block a single access point, or just need to stand in front of one bus, you may not need an extensive communications network. However, it is much more likely that your people will be spread out and you will need to co-ordinate and respond to changing conditions. Each group of your people should have a cell phone or walkie-talkie, and ideally one person in each group should have the sole role of staying on that line. Remember that cell phones can be jammed and, if you have the people, have some dedicated to serving as runners, going back and forth and keeping your teams informed. *Tip:* Know your local laws. While the people serving on the blockade are almost certain to be breaking the law, the people serving as runners (staying on public space such as sidewalks, and not impeding anyone) may be able to help without breaking the law. This doesn't mean they won't get harassed by the cops (in fact, their mobility makes interference more likely) but knowing your rights will serve you well when things go bad.

Team upkeep: If you only need to block your target for a few hours, sanitation may not be an issue, but if you need to be in place for an extended period of time the basics of life can become a problem. Unlike other, less confrontational protest types, with a blockade you can expect no support or services either from your target or from the city. You are on your own, and should plan accordingly. Some basics:

Food/drink: It is easier to scream on a full stomach. If you plan to be in place for longer than a few hours you need to plan for food and drink for your people. Everyone should be carrying protest packs with food bars and water, but this will only last for a day or so. If you are going to be in place longer (for example, having you and your team sitting in a historic building to stop it being bulldozed) you need to pack quite a bit more food. When packing your equipment before the protest, pack enough food to feed all your people, plus a little extra to supply sympathetic people who join your cause (it can happen) for at least a few days longer than you plan to be in place. So if you want to be in place for a week leading up to a city council meeting you want to have enough food to cover at least ten days.

For open-ended protests where you don't know how long you will have to be in place (but don't expect it to be short) food becomes a much bigger issue. In addition to taking food in with you initially, you may need to be re-supplied as the protest goes on. Your target (and the cops) know this, and are likely to try to hamper efforts to keep you supplied.

One solution is to hide in plain sight. Protests draw crowds, and you may be able to get food in by having someone hide in the crowd and toss in a backpack of food and supplies. Done quickly and quietly they can be gone before anyone notices you chowing down. If you vary the times you do this, the people doing the deliveries, and the way they dress, you can keep supplied for quite a long while.

Alternately you can try to sneak food in, usually at night when no one is looking. This is a bit riskier and harder to pull off, but for protests that are more isolated (such as tree sitting) this may be your only option. Try to sneak in a wave of several people so that if you do get seen you can all rush in at once, almost ensuring that some food gets through. Done properly you can keep your protesters fed indefinitely.

A more extreme alternative is to add a hunger strike to your protest. Hunger strikes serve many purposes — to show your dedication to your cause, to draw public attention, and to shame your target into action. This should not be done without proper thought (people can and do die during hunger strikes) but it may serve as a way to eliminate the food issue.

With food and drink taken care of your next obvious problem is sanitation. For short protests of a few hours you may not have to worry about rest rooms (everyone went before we came, right?) but if you plan to be in place even for a full day this becomes an issue. You can't exactly go in public (not even sneaking into an alley for a moment, since the cops will want to bust you for everything they can). If you shut down a building entrance or other area near an interior restroom you may be able to use that, but for the most part the solution for rest rooms is bring-your-own. A large tarp for privacy and a bucket or three are required gear, and you'll need to plan for a place to store your waste. And of course, remember that toilet paper!

Dress: The main reason for protests is usually to raise public awareness and shape public opinion. If your blockade occurs where the public can see you, consider wearing clothing or signs with your issue written on them. You want people walking by to see you and know immediately why you are going to this extreme.

Maintaining the blockade: Blockades are all about getting in someone's way, and when you do that people tend to want to move you. Your target will try everything to get you to move, from talking you out of your blockade to threats to direct action. You may be resolute in your convictions but make no mistake about it, someone in a three-ton bulldozer screaming about running you over is quite intimidating.

The screaming and threats are to be expected, but there are ways to defend yourself from the direct action. Often the most effective way to keep your target under control is to make sure the media is there in force. Someone who might be willing to lose it and beat the shit out of you may not be willing to do so knowing it will make the eleven o'clock news.

If you are too far off the beaten path, or in a long-term protest where the media won't always be there, you may need to bring your own media. If some members of your team have video cameras, and make that fact clear to your target, it may deter them. Of course, when tensions run high, people can be irrational, camera in their face or no. The risks are very real, and any protester putting themselves in harms way must be aware of them. As an extreme example, Rachael Corrie flew all the way from Washington state to protest Israeli occupation of Palestine. Her camera, and those of her fellow protesters did not save her from her fate. On March 16, 2003, an Israeli bulldozer driver, who may well have seen her, drove over her, killing her. The goal of every protester should be to create change, to speak out and be heard, not to die for the cause.

While your target may not legally be able to use force to move you, the cops most certainly can. You may be able to delay the cops from acting by weight of numbers (one cop in a squad car isn't equipped to deal with three dozen chanting protesters) and (as the WTO demonstrated) if the cops are overwhelmed and too busy to devote the manpower for arrests you may buy even more time. However, if the cops decide to arrest you they will usually have the resources to do so. You basically have two options once that happens. One is to comply and get arrested. You don't have to comply with an order to disperse, but once they come in to get you and cart you away you may want to go limp and let them haul you off (again try to get arrested on camera).

The other option is passive resistance. There are a variety of ways to make yourself hard to arrest, and this will be determined mostly by the site you are protesting at. If you want to go this route, mapping out your target ahead of time is a must.

66

From sitting so high in a tree you can't be brought down, to chaining yourself to the door, your goal is to make yourself hard to remove.

There are two concerns with this you need to think of. First off, if you tie yourself down you lose mobility and will create problems (it is hard to go to the bathroom tied to a door). This inconvenience is secondary to the risk you place yourself at by not being able to get out and flee if things go badly. If you are tied in one place and you get tear-gassed you are in for a very unpleasant few hours. This may be acceptable, but know what you are in for ahead of time. You may also want to try to tie yourself in such a way that you keep one hand free.

There are too many ways to tie yourself down to go into here. If you plan to go this route do some homework ahead of time, look up any of the several works on getting yourself locked in one place, and practice, practice, practice. As an extra security precaution you may want to have one of your people who is not participating directly in the blockade stay in the background with the keys to your handcuffs or locks just in case they are needed.

After the Blockade

Like all protests, it is very important to look back after your protest and analyze how effective you have been. Here are some of the things you'll want to look at after your protest.

The first thing to note is that as blockades are highly confrontational and usually illegal, you are likely to be doing this analysis from a jail cell, so you want to ensure you have appropriate legal support. You want to have lawyers and bail bondsmen lined up ahead of time, and now you need to get them into play to help you and your people. It may also be useful to have lawyers who are willing to be on camera after the event to speak to the media on your behalf. Blockades are often less about shaping public opinion than other protests, but a good media image never hurts.

In the worst-case scenario of mass arrests and long-term detentions, lawyers can also be critical for getting information between jailed members of your team. Try to find a lawyer who will represent all of your people and can keep you all informed of developments both in your case and of the results of your protest.

Once you get your legal needs taken care of, you can get into the real analysis of your actions. One primary advantage blockades have over other protests is that you have clear immediate results. While most protests look to shape public opinion, which can be hard to judge, a blockade looks to do something direct in the short term. Did the conference shut down? Is the forest still standing? Did the mayor decide not to show up? In short, did you accomplish your goal?

If not, you want to look at what went wrong, from quicker than anticipated police intervention to a breakdown in the blockade itself. If you did accomplish your goal the most critical thing is to look at your target's response. If you shut down a meeting on Saturday, and they just reschedule and run their meeting on Sunday, you may not be having the impact you want. Large events (such as conferences or public hearings) require quite a bit of logistic work and communications to get them set up, and you can expect that your target will not be able to quickly reschedule a large conference, but if it is just a few senior executives at a company, they can just meet in a different building (or with a few days and a few quick plane reservations, a different state) and avoid you. If you can get information about where this new meeting will take place (and they will try to prevent you from getting this information) you might try to shut it down as well. Otherwise you may just want to be satisfied knowing you have disrupted their plans and hopefully made your point.

Overall, blockades are one of the most confrontational, complicated, and chaotic of protests but as for results blockades can be relied on to have a lasting impact.

Blockade variant: Invasions. One slightly lower risk variant of blockades is the invasion, getting a large group of people to invade an area (an office or lobby, for example) and protest. Having two dozen people chanting and dancing in their lobby will make your target pay attention, and you retain the ability to bail out when your risk tolerance is exceeded (such as when the carloads of cops show up).

Blockade Checklist:

Personnel:
- [ ] Media liaison
- [ ] Lawyer(s)
- [ ] Medical personnel
- [ ] Runners (if blocking multiple areas)

Toys:
- [ ] Locks/chains (with keys)
- [ ] Maps of the target and blockade points
- [ ] Still/video cameras
- [ ] Food/water (for long term blockades)

What Has Come Before:
Protests in History

Not all blockades occur on land. In 1971 protesters allied with the Movement for a New Society held one of the most well-organized and effective blockades to protest U.S. arms exports to West Pakistan during the civil war with East Pakistan. In addition to marches and picket lines, protesters in canoes and small craft physically blocked Pakistani freighters, and succeeded in blockading Philadelphia's port, preventing weapon shipments until the end of the war in 1972.

This success was in part due to the Movement's work to educate and join forces with other groups, such as the longshoremen who refused to load Pakistani ships. The broad alliance of people the Movement created enabled them to hold one of the most successful nonviolent blockades in history.

Chapter Eight
Protest Highlight: Letter Campaigns

Letter writing campaigns are a very effective way to show widespread support and interest in your cause, and serve as a call to action directed at your target that can be more effective in creating change than other protest methods. The key idea of a letter writing campaign is to organize members of the public to write and send letters (lots of letters) indicating your position and the change you want to see happen. They are often directed at government officials to influence an upcoming vote or policy decision, but they also have been used for everything from asking corporate CEOs to end child labor to making university administrators aware of the effect of a budget cut on students.

Running a letter writing campaign has a number of advantages over other forms of protest.

Unlike protests that are (or can become) illegal, letter campaigns are fully legal, with most participants risking nothing more hazardous than a paper cut. Asking people to join you in the streets asks them to place themselves at some risk, but asking them to write a letter is usually pretty safe. In addition, by working "within the system" you gain an air of respectability. Many people may view protesters in the streets as rabble-rousers and malcontents that they cannot relate to, but everyone has written a letter.

An effective letter writing campaign will also have the effect of carrying the weight of a large community of people. While a politician may want to ignore a line of protesters outside his office it is harder to ignore hundreds of letters dropped on his desk every day. Politicians need voters. Corporations need consumers. They will respond to the voice of the people they rely on to continue to exist.

Letter campaigns are also very effective for creating clear short-term change. While other protests may serve to raise awareness or protest large actions (such as an anti-war march) letter campaigns demand clear, direct action: a vote, a change in wages, a direct change in policy. By being focused on a clear, easily expressed short-term goal, letter campaigns can accomplish what other protests cannot.

Of course letter campaigns come with their own difficulties. If you are thinking of protesting this way, here are some things to think of:

One downside of sending hundreds or thousands of letters is that all those letters need stamps, envelopes, and so on. While each letter doesn't cost much, it adds up. There are ways to reduce this cost, but letter campaigns can prove much more expensive than other protests. Sit-ins are free. Stamps are not.

You can help reduce the cost in several ways. One is to give out letters and trust the public to stamp their own envelope, thus cutting your postage cost to zero. This may look attractive, but it will cost you in effectiveness. The more you ask members of the public to do, the fewer will follow through and the less effective you will be. Since the whole point of a letter campaign is to send huge waves of letters you want to do everything you can to maximize the number of letters you can send. Instead of asking people to stamp their own envelopes, you are much better off having pre-stamped envelopes to put the letters in and asking for a donation for postage as people write the letters. This probably won't fully cover your postage and other costs, but it will help.

Another way to cut costs may be to send postcards instead of letters. Postcards are cheaper to mail, and people can write them faster, but you add the cost of the postcards themselves. Making your own pre-printed postcards is more difficult and time consuming than just using envelopes, but you gain the impact of being able to place an image of your choice on the front. (Be sure to use an image the post office will permit. If you use an image that is too graphic the USPS may cut you off before you ever reach your target.) Your local phone book should list several print shops that can help you print your own postcards, and some may be willing to cut you a price break if they can put their name and phone number on the card.

If you have the time and can fulfill the requirements you might want to register your group as a non-profit organization and look into getting bulk rates for mailings.

Another issue that letter campaigns run into is ignorability. Most letters have to pass through quite a few people before reaching their intended recipient. A secretary can toss your letters before they are even read by the person you want to influence. One of the functions of secretaries is to screen out mail that decision makers receive, to allow them to focus on only what matters. Those secretaries may not share your view of what's important.

You don't know in advance what opinions the people who get your letters will hold, but you can render them less important by sheer weight of numbers. While a gatekeeper may toss one letter, or a dozen, if they get hundreds of letters a day they have no choice but to make sure this comes to the attention of the people you are trying to talk to. Similarly, they may choose to ignore a few letters, but if they come to work every morning and have to pick through waves and waves of letters all on the same issue it becomes very difficult to ignore.

In addition to these issues, letter campaigns also can be more time-consuming than other protests. You can (if you have to) take to the streets on a few hours notice, you can start a sit-in with only a few phone calls, but moving things through the Postal Service is not exactly known to be swift. Getting the community involved, getting letters written, and getting them to your target all take time. That time can be minimized if you plan efficiently, but the time issue is a fact of letter campaigns. If you don't have at least a few weeks of time to execute your protest this may not be the protest type for you.

As with all protests, the effectiveness of letter campaigns depends on the planning and effort you put into it. Here are some of the steps needed to run an effective letter campaign.

Planning/Preparation for the Protest

The most important decision you have to make in a letter campaign is, do you write the letter yourself in full or do you supply key points to the public and let them write letters in their own words? Both can be effective, but in different ways. If you write the letters out in full yourself you will probably send more letters, as people need do no more than sign their name and mail the letters. However, if every letter your target gets reads the same then your protest is basically a large, attention getting petition, lacking individual human character. In addition, if every letter your target receives reads the same they will stop reading them. They may still be impressed by the quantity of letters, of public interest, but the personal touch is lost. Going this route trades quality of letters for quantity, and that may hurt your overall effect.

By asking people to take your key points and write letters in their own words you are asking for more effort (and will get less letters) but these personalized letters carry more weight, saying, "Look, I care enough about this issue to write this letter, to put down my concern and bring it to your attention. Deal with me." If you are willing to put in the effort to ensure your quantity of letters is high enough, individual letters will be much more effective overall. You may also want to try doing both, asking people to write letters on the spot at tables while handing out (or mailing) blank letters for people who can't be at your tables while they are set up.

Either way, the first thing you have to do is some writing, either writing the letter itself, or writing the bullet points for others to write their letters from. Spend some time on this, show it around, and work to get the writing as effective and clear as you can. Some research here will pay off with the buzzwords and lingo you'll need to use. If the letter itself doesn't read well, if people don't understand the bullet points you give them, the rest of the protest will collapse.

Once you get your writing ready, confirm the address you are sending them to. It may seem like an obvious point, but you need to make sure not only that you have the correct address, but that it is the most effective address to use. Writing your congressman? If his office has a direct address you can use to avoid going through a central post office you can reach him faster. And why not direct some of the mail to his home address? Once you have the addresses you want to use, confirm them. Make sure you have the right address, check it, then have someone else check it again. All your effort is for nothing if you mail hundreds of letters to a bad address.

The next step is to collect the supplies you'll need. In addition to copies of the letter/bullet points, you need pre-stamped envelopes, lots of pens and paper for people to write letters with, and some promotional letters or business cards for your group with contact information. You may want to include a selection of different types and sizes of paper and envelopes to enhance the individual look and feel of each letter.

Once you get set up you need to go out and get the people to write the letters and get them sent off. You have to make a decision as to how you plan to get people to write these letters. You can hand out packets of information with your bullet points and pre-stamped envelopes, which may let you reach a larger group of people (you could even mail these packets out and reach people you never see) but which may produce fewer letters to your target for each information packet you make. People are more likely to blow you off, forget to mail letters, or otherwise not follow through if there is a time delay and you are no longer with them. You trade easier distribution for fewer letters overall. If you go this route, the most critical thing for you to have is a Web site with sample letters and bullet points for people, so that you can hand out and put up small stickers with the URL.

Alternatively you can set up a booth or table in a public space and ask people to sign or write letters right on the spot. This gives you more direct contact with the public, and lets you get more people to follow through and write letters. You need to supply people a place to sit and write, as well as the bullet points to build a letter from and perhaps some sample letters. You should provide several different sample letters in different formats both to ensure people find a letter type they will feel comfortable working from and to ensure that your target gets letters that don't all read the same. You also want to make sure, once people start writing that you get the letter then. If they walk away to finish the letter "later" odds are it will never be sent.

While you have their attention, you should also supply people with a signup list where they can give you their e-mail address, phone number, or other contact information. People willing to take the time and effort to sit and write out a letter on your issue may serve as valuable allies in later protests, and with a contact list you can let them know about the results after the protest is over. Some people won't feel comfortable signing, especially if your issue is particularly controversial, and you should respect that, but get the contact information for those that will give it to you.

The other upside of setting up a table for people to write at is that as you collect letters you can hit them up for a small donation to help cover your costs, postage and so on. You don't want to be overly pushy, but by reminding them that all those stamps cost money when mailing their letters is in the front of their minds, you will generate more donations than just asking for money without showing a clear need.

You can either decide to set your table up until you have a certain number of letters (200, for example), or put it up for a certain length of time (say, a week) and send as many letters as you get. If you choose the latter, plan to stay set up later if you find you don't get as many letters as you want. Once you have the letters, spread out your mailings. If you have several hundred letters (a good target number for a small letter protest), mail a dozen or so each day so that your target gets enough each day to be impressed, and keep them coming for as long as possible in order to keep your issue on the agenda of your target. For example, if your target is a public official and you want them to vote a certain way in an upcoming vote you might try to start hitting them two weeks ahead of time with a few dozen letters a day, then ramp up with more letters in the last few days before the vote.

In addition to the letters you are writing to your target you also want to send letters to the editor of all your local papers. These do not need to be anywhere near the quantity that you are sending your target, and you can write them yourself instead of prompting the public to write them, but by making sure your local papers get three or four letters a week you can get letters into the paper calling for the public to join you in writing to your target. These letters to the editor also raise awareness about your issues, and can be used to promote a Web site or other ways for people to get more information.

Follow Up

As with all protests, what you do after the protest is almost as important as the protest itself. Letter campaigns are very useful when you want to create very specific change, and whether you get the result you want or not you need to follow up both with your target and with the community that is impacted by the result.

If your goal is to create a change that can be measured in the short term (a vote, a decision about where to place a factory or a waste dump) then you should follow up with your target, call them up and thank them for their action, or remind them that their actions will be remembered. That little act, the simple action of contacting and creating another level to the relationship between you and your target, can pay off a great deal in the long term. If you got what you wanted you can thank your target for their action, and lay the groundwork for additional contact down the road. If you didn't get what you want you can make sure your target knows you are still watching, and when you protest again (with letters or in other ways) your impact will be greater as it builds on what you have already done.

The additional value to this simple act of contact is to remind your target that you will still be watching them. If you convince a politician to vote for a bill to create a homeless shelter, when you call up to thank him for his vote you can mention (politely) that you'll be following this bill through the budget process and to the actual creation of the shelter. By keeping your eyes on the process you help avoid having all your work negated in some committee.

In addition to your original target, you also want to follow up with the community. No matter what the result, you should use the contact information that people gave you to let them know what the result of their action has been. In success congratulate them, and thank them for their help. In failure remind them of why you took action in the first place. If you plan protests of another type this is the best way to get people to rally to your cause. Remind people of what the next step is, be it to look forward to the opening of the shelter or the next vote. The important thing is to keep them informed and involved.

Variants

This protest method is ultimately based on massive waves of communications to your target, and of course, there are more ways to do that than mailing letters. Here are some variants for the letter campaign, and the ups and downs of each.

Phone banks: Almost every politician has at least one public phone number, and a little legwork can get you a number for almost anyone, from corporate CEOs to the Chief of Police. Distributing this number with a sheet of bullet point information can let people contact your target themselves, on their own time, over the course of several days. You can also set up a phone tree so that once you have the right contact information it can be distributed (along with any other relevant information) to everyone you are working with, easily and without too much effort by any one person.

One note for phone campaigns: Check the phone number. There's no point in handing out cards with a number that doesn't connect to your target (and include those area codes). Call the number yourself right before the protest, and at least every few days during the protest. If your target really doesn't want to deal with you they can have that number disconnected, or set it to a voicemail that never gets answered.

Advantages:

Personal touch: Conversations are inherently more personal, and you can convey the importance of your issue and the strength of your convictions more fully when people can hear your voice.

Ease of use: Asking people to write a letter involves much more effort and time than just picking up the phone and calling. The easier you make things for the public the more people you can expect to get working with you.

Speed: Letters take time to reach their target. If you need to make your target aware of your displeasure and try to get them to change actions quickly, phone campaigns can help you create change quickly.

Disadvantages:

Lower public response: Every time you ask the public to take more and more direct effort, the fewer will actually do so. Writing a letter is one thing, actually calling someone and talking is something else, and something many people may not be comfortable doing. If you distribute cards with the phone number and a few bullet points about your issue and you get even a small percentage of people to actually call you're doing pretty well. You can mitigate this somewhat by setting up a phone bank to let people call from a central location, but then you lose the effect of having the calls spread over several days, and your costs can go up.

Cost: A letter costs just a few cents, but a phone call, especially if you are calling long distance, can add up quite a bit. You can spread this cost among many people by asking each person to make a phone call of just a few minutes on their own line, thus spreading the cost. Also, progressive long distance phone companies like Working Assets (www.workingassets.com) provide free long distance minutes each month to call public officials.

E-mail campaigns: The high-tech, modern variant of the letter writing campaign, e-mail campaigns seek to deluge your target's inbox instead of their mailbox. This can be very attractive as a protest under the right conditions, but has its own unique downsides. E-mail campaigns can either work as traditional letter campaigns (write this message to this address) or work as a sign-on letter (add your name to the bottom of this list and forward it; every 50th person should send it to this address).

Advantages:

Speed: E-mail gets from you to your target more or less instantly. For protests where you do not have very long to impact your target, waiting for letters to work their way through the mail may not be an option.

Cost: E-mail has basically a zero incremental cost. Once you go to the effort to get the right e-mail address and promote that to the public (which can also be done at least partially online) the cost per e-mail is zero.

Disadvantages:

Public tech savvyness: It is very easy for people who are online all the time to forget that many people still do not use computers regularly. If you use this as your only method of contacting your target (instead of, in conjunction with, a letter campaign) you lose members of the public who are uncomfortable with or unable to use e-mail.

Ignorability: Even more so than letters, e-mail can be ignored. Your target can delete hundreds of e-mails unread with the click of a mouse. Even worse, if your target knows a bit about computers (or has an IT department that does) they can set their servers to route all e-mail to a specific address, or all e-mail with a keyword in the subject line, directly to the trash (although many of these systems will tally keywords within the e-mails, so at least you can get numbers of support on your side). Not only can your target ignore your e-mails, but they can set it up so they never see them in the first place.

Impact: E-mail simply doesn't have the physical impact of other methods of protest. Opening your inbox and finding 20 e-mails is not as impressive as getting 20 phone calls or finding 20 letters waiting on your desk in a pile. In addition, people are conditioned to think of unwanted e-mail as Spam, junk that can be safely ignored.

Any of these protest types can be effective in getting the results you want. More important than the method of contacting your target is the effort you put in and the numbers of people you get writing or calling with you. Get out there, and good luck.

Letter Checklist:

Personnel:
- ☐ Media liaison
- ☐ Company/target liaison
- ☐ People to set up and work the table

Toys:
- ☐ Envelopes (pre-addressed with confirmed address)
- ☐ Stamps
- ☐ Table space to distribute from
- ☐ Sample letters (3 or more)

What Has Come Before: Protests in History

Perhaps the most well-known organization working on letter writing campaigns is Amnesty International. With members all over the world writing thousands of letters a year, AI works to free political prisoners and prisoners of conscience of all types. These campaigns can pay off; in 1993, General Gallardo was jailed for criticizing the Mexican military on human rights violations and for proposing the creation of an ombudsman to oversee military human rights issues. AI picked up the cause in 1994, and after years of work and thousands of letters Mexican President Fox reduced the sentence to time served and let Gallardo go. He and his family said that without AI and the international attention they brought he may never have been released.

Chapter Nine
Protest Highlight: Boycotts

Sometimes protesting is a complicated act, requiring long logistical planning and risky personal interaction. But sometimes protest, and change, can require nothing more than picking up a different box of cereal or drinking a different cup of coffee. Boycotts, the act of collectively choosing not to buy a product or not to use a service, act as a direct way to communicate with your target and indicate your displeasure. Corporations who will ignore marchers in the streets and hang up on angry callers have no choice but to deal with you when their monthly profit statements start to bleed red ink.

Boycotts have been popular all through history as an effective way to communicate displeasure to a target. The term itself dates from a protest in the 1880s when tenant farmers in Ireland fought oppression from an unreasonable landholder by refusing to have any economic or social dealings with him or his family. His name? Captain Charles Boycott.

Boycotts can be very effective, but in many ways are more complex and more difficult to pull off successfully than most other protest types. Successful boycotts have two advantages over other protest types: direct economic impact on your target, and an increase in public awareness about your issue (without which a boycott cannot have impact). However, to get those effects, boycotts require a great deal of work. Compared to other protests, boycotts require more time and energy from you and far more public commitment (and the effort to get them committed) than any other protest. If you are marching in the street, sending out letters, or getting on the news, you are just telling the public, "Here's what up. This is going on, and you should be aware of this." With a boycott you are asking them not only to become informed (hard enough) but also to take action themselves. The weight of public opinion is never easy to move, but when it gets rolling it is very hard to stop.

Planning a boycott starts, as with all protests, with having a clear goal. It is vitally important that you know what change you want to bring about, in as specific of terms as possible, before you move forward. If your concern is a local restaurant that is discriminating against African Americans, is your goal to have them hire more African Americans managers? To offer compensation to African Americans who have been discriminated against? Do you just want them shut down and out of the community? You are going to be communicating with the public to get them on your side, and without a clear goal to set them towards, boycotts become very vague, idea-based actions, and the public is far less likely to give you the support you are going to require.

Once you have your clear goal in mind, it is time to do some homework. You are going to be asking the public not to do something (shop at a particular store, buy a particular laundry detergent) and if you expect people to do this you need to provide alternatives. A little time spent here can make or break your protest. Every time you ask people to change their behavior patterns you ask them to expend energy, time, and thought dealing with something that often is simply off their radar. The less effort they have to expend to support your boycott, the more people are likely to help your cause. If all you are asking is that they choose the detergent on the top shelf instead of the one on the middle shelf, it is a simple change for them. If you are asking them to go all the way across town instead of shopping right down the block you will find many fewer people willing to make the effort. If it is a big enough issue, something they can relate with, they may be willing to go quite far out of their way, but the easier you make it for them to support you, the better. In addition, try to keep the focus of your boycott narrow. Asking people to boycott a specific product or service is one thing, asking them to boycott the whole PepsiCo empire — Pepsi itself, Frito Lay (Doritos, Fritos), Quaker Oats (Gatorade, Cap'n Crunch) Aquafina water, Dole juice, Tropicana, the list goes on — is quite another.

With your clear goal and selected alternatives in hand, another thing to consider is your impact on your target. A protest should usually be used as a last resort, and every effort should be made to create change in less confrontational ways, but marchers in the street or letters in the mail are unlikely to put anyone out of business. If your target is a large corporation such as Philip Morris and you want to protest their cigarette advertising you can be sure that while you will have impact you are unlikely to see them go away. But if your target is, as in the above example, a local restaurant discriminating against blacks, the economic impact of a boycott lasting even a few months could put them completely out of business. If that's your goal, fine, but if you just want them to change their ways you may want to warn them ahead of time of your plans for a boycott as a final attempt to strong-arm them into change. Your target may be pissing you off, but an empty storefront doesn't do your community any good either.

Finally, one often-overlooked aspect of boycotts is the need to have a good exit strategy, a plan for when you can stop. Asking people to forever change how they do things is a big request, but just changing behavior for a day may not have the impact you want. The time you need to make your message heard will be different for each boycott, but you should know the point in time (or the event) that means your boycott is over.

Usually this end point will be time-based. If you want students to boycott a school cafeteria, a single day may be all you need, with the sight of all those empty chairs and unpurchased burgers making your point. If you want to protest a national chain of hotdogs for how they are slaughtering their animals you may need to boycott for a month, or longer, to have an economic impact they will notice.

One very good strategy for timing your protest is to tie it to an event or holiday. Asking people to boycott Wendy's restaurants for their anti-gay actions (such as when they pulled advertising dollars from the Ellen Degeneres show after the lead actor came out) may reach a wider audience and stay in people's minds more if you ask them to boycott specifically during Gay Pride Week. Asking people to not buy turkey from a national farm that treats its animals inhumanely will have more resonance (and perhaps more impact) if timed around Thanksgiving, when turkeys are in people's minds anyway.

Alternately you may choose to boycott until your target changes their ways, or does something specific. In the turkey example above you might choose to boycott until they move to free range farming for turkeys and take them out of the small cages most are now raised in. This is a noble goal, but what do you do if your target doesn't comply? Continue your protest indefinitely? This may work for you (many vegetarians are basically boycotting meat on ethical grounds and have done so for years) but asking the public to forever change their ways is quite another thing. In addition if you come out and say, "We will boycott until this change is made," and it is never made, if (or when) your boycott ends you risk giving your target the impression that you aren't serious and you don't represent the real public opinion and a real threat. Boycott "to the end" can work, but know what you are letting yourself in for.

No matter how you plan to end your boycott, the timeline for your protest is a key element you need to communicate to the public. If they feel you are asking them to forever give up something they value they are less likely to support you. If they know it has a clear timeline the pressure on them is lower. This is the idea behind campaigns asking people to take public transportation or bike to work one day a week (in effect boycotting their own cars, and the related gas and oil industries). If you asked people to give up their cars they'd laugh you out the door (and possibly off the North American continent). If you are only asking them to ride public transportation on Mondays in April, people can go, ok, it is a small request, I'll try it out. However your boycott is structured you need to know (and be able to communicate to the public) when your boycott will end.

Once you have your protest in place and get the boycott underway, the most important thing to do to maintain the boycott is communication. Boycotts last longer than most other protests and require far more public participation to succeed. The quality of your communications with the public, and with your target, will determine if your boycott has the desired effect or not.

The first person you want to talk to is your target. If your target is local you may want to warn them to try to get them to change their ways and avoid the protest entirely. If your target is a multinational corporation or other huge monstrosity you want to alert them right before your action so your effect isn't brushed off as a seasonal drop in sales or other anomaly. Be clear in your communications with your target, state your goals and why you are taking action, and offer ideas for how they can comply with your requests. If you are boycotting Nike to protest sweatshop labor do your homework and list the pay rates for workers and the price of Nike shoes in your local store and include this information as a reason for your protest. Ask for clear action from your target, perhaps asking Nike to raise pay rates in Third World countries to a living wage.

Once your target knows that your boycott is coming you have the hardest part of the whole protest, communicating your ideas and goals to the public. More than any other protest, for a boycott you have to have the public not only interested in your cause but on your side enough to take action (even if the action is just picking up a different box of cereal).

How you communicate your message to the public will of course, vary based on who you are dealing with, but the media is going to be a very important aid for you. Media coverage, and coverage with a positive spin, is critical. You need to go beyond the press releases and phone calls that might be all you need to give the media for other protests, and actively try to speak with reporters and editors and get articles about your upcoming boycott. Write letters to the editor. Call local radio stations. Get your message out.

The most effective and direct way to get people to change their actions is to talk to them at the point of that action. Boycotts require a great deal of time and people because you need to have your people at the point of action asking people to support your boycott. This will be your main communication with the public.

You need to try to be as close to the point of action as possible when you ask people to act. If you are boycotting a restaurant you can stand outside the main doors. If you are boycotting a product on store shelves you may not be able to stand right by the product. When you can't be right there to ask for action as people make their choice you need to get as close as you can. With a product in a store you might set up a booth outside and hand out flyers shoppers can carry with them. Give people something to take with them and keep your boycott in their minds. You can also take several (less legal) steps, such as printing up stickers making your case (now with 25% more dead dolphins!) and sticking them on the products on store shelves. One way or another, you have to be talking to the public at the point of action. If you call them up ahead of time, or send out letters, or post posters, but don't communicate with them as they act, as they buy something, or use a service, then it will be very hard to have any real impact.

One other thing boycotts have that other protests do not is intermediaries, people you need to communicate with, and that you may hurt in the crossfire, who are not directly connected to your goals. If you are boycotting Nike, and choose to set up shop outside of Foot Locker stores, Foot Locker is going to be worried about your actions. For the most part, these people are going to be innocents, people who are just trying to make a living. It can be argued that they are as responsible as the people you are targeting (Nike could not sell shoes without distributors) but the public is unlikely to see it that way, and as your boycott can have direct impact on their ability to stay in business they are going to be some of the primary people fighting your boycott.

You can save yourself a great deal of grief by trying to deal with this conflict ahead of time. If you want to do damage to the intermediaries and don't mind the economic impact on them, that's one thing, but you may find they can help your cause. Identify the intermediaries your boycott will affect, find what their motives are (usually money) and see if you can find a way to help them while serving your boycott. A local store selling Nabisco products that you are boycotting might be willing to do additional displays and supply more shelf space for the organic cookies and crackers you are suggesting people buy instead. The more people you can get to work with you instead of against you, the more impact you can have.

Avoiding as much conflict as you can becomes even more important in longer-term boycotts. Boycotts are very labor intensive and if all of your people get arrested for trespassing in the first hour you are going to have a very short, very ignorable protest.

During the boycott itself there is quite a bit more to worry about than just "don't buy X." One is the "bubble effect," the tendency of people not to want to go against the crowd, to not want to be the first to do something. You want to create the visual effect that people are participating in your boycott, and you can have problems if there is a visible example of people not doing so. If you are boycotting a restaurant and people look past your signs at nothing but empty tables they are unlikely to want to be the first to sit down. Once a few tables fill up, the bubble is broken and it is easier for people to ignore you and sit down themselves. In some cases there is nothing you can do to mitigate this effect, but if you are creative and think on your feet you can at least lower the visual impact. If people are sitting in a booth at the restaurant you are boycotting get a nice big sign explaining the boycott and use it to block the window to the booth they are sitting at. If a few people buy the product you are boycotting, rearrange the remaining products on store shelves to create the impression nothing has been sold. Little touches go a long way to maintaining the mental bubble and making people unwilling to be the first to break the boycott.

With that in mind, it is also important to keep up your own morale over the long term of the protest. If you take every purchase of the boycotted product as a personal defeat you risk burning out, getting desperate and losing your effectiveness. All you can do is supply information and suggest action to the public. Your goal need not be zero usage of the product in question. If your target sees sales drop 40% because of your action you can be assured they will take notice. Stay focused on the long-term goal.

On the subject of morale, you are almost certainly going to come in contact, and conflict, with the members of the public who, in spite of your boycott, continue to use the product or service of your target. For whatever reason (brand loyalty, perceived need, or just sheer habit) some people will ignore what you are trying to do. You want to reach out to these people, talk to them, tell them what you are doing and why, but you MUST NOT act to antagonize them. These people are not the enemy. If you make them think about what they are doing they may change. If you make them feel like shit they are going to tune you out. Stay vocal, and stay loud, but stay civil, at least with the public.

Once you reach the end point for your boycott your work isn't over yet. You still have two key tasks: Thanking the public and explaining their impact, and making sure your target knows what you've done and what you are willing to do in the future.

If you can produce clear numbers to show the success of your boycott (lost sales dollars, poor event attendance, low ratings or circulation numbers) you should trumpet your success in the media and local organizations and get the word out to the public what they have helped to do. Use this opportunity to let them know how they can contact you and help with future protests if any are needed. Make sure anyone who has questions about what happened can contact you and get your side of the story, because they will certainly be able to contact your target. This is even more important if there was major conflict, police intervention or other happenings that may reflect negatively on your protest in the public eye.

Next you need to contact your target and make sure they fully understand what you've done. Even if you think you've left them no way to ignore you, make sure that once you are off their porch you are not out of their minds. Whether you've done a great deal of damage or not, as soon as your boycott is over you should thank them for any concessions they've made, and if you have not gotten the results you want you should explain that you are not going away. If a one-day boycott didn't have the result you want, perhaps a week will, or another type of protest (it is hard to eat in a restaurant with someone chained to the door). You want to avoid threatening your target (both because you don't want to give them specific things to defend against and because it may well be illegal) but you want to remind them that you (and many like you) are still concerned with the issue. Again provide the information you gave them at the beginning about specific ways they can change and how to do so. Once you've enhanced your credibility with a successful boycott they will look at your request in a new light. And if they still don't comply with your requests, well, then it is back to the streets.

Boycott Checklist:

Personnel:
- ☐ Media liaison
- ☐ Company/target liaison
- ☐ People to talk to the public

Toys:
- ☐ Signs/stickers
- ☐ Product alternatives

What Has Come Before: Protests in History

Boycotts create change, but often they take time to work. The AFL-CIO maintains many boycotts, one of which recently claimed a victory. A 22-year, national boycott of the San Francisco Marriott Hotel ended with new contracts granting employees an average 3% wage increase, health insurance premium payment, child and elder care benefit payments, and profit sharing or pension options. Without the union involvement and the show of solidarity and economic impact of the long-term boycott this progress would have been impossible.

Chapter Ten
A Sample Protest

Nothing can prepare you for running a protest more effectively than experience, and you should try to get involved with as many protests as you can, but a few in-depth examples will help give you some tips on what to expect. Here is a sample protest, from conception to results.

As a sample group of protesters, let us take a group of students from the University of Washington's School of Social Work. These students have been studying the difficulties of living on minimum wage and find out that a vote in the state government to raise the minimum wage looks like it will fail. They want to get some public attention drawn to the vote and encourage the legislators to raise the minimum wage.

The first thing to do, of course, is to determine what type of protest to have, and to do that they have to assess the resources at their disposal. They have two dozen or so students, all very fired up about this issue, they have the university's computers, Internet access and printing, and they have a few weeks before the vote to plan.

With those resources, what kind of protest should they hold? A sit-in at the capitol would draw lots of media attention but may be too confrontational, not only because of the probability of arrest but also because the university may take issue with having its name associated with such action. A letter writing campaign is a popular and low conflict way to talk to government, but there may not be enough time to hold one, and besides the students want to be more active than just writing letters.

In the end the students decide that they want to hold a march, running from the university campus to downtown, so they can end with a rally outside the main shopping district. With that set, they can get down to planning the details of the march.

The first thing they do is plan the route they want to take and send a representative to the local city permit agency to apply for a permit to march. While it is possible to march without a permit and permission, the students decide that conflict would just distract from the message they are trying to convey. One of the students is chosen to be the representative to the government so that there is always one person dealing consistently with the government bureaucracy, and they call up the city council offices and find the correct place to apply for a permit.

They need a nice large place to begin the march, to let people show up early, get together and get organized in the morning. They also need a nice large space to end up accommodating all the marchers, as well as anyone they have picked up on the way and any media. Not wanting to reinvent the wheel, they look at what protests in the past have done. In Seattle, on the UW campus, Red Square has always been a prime protest gathering point, and has all the space they need. Winding out of campus and heading downtown they can end up in Westlake Park, right in the heart of the shopping district, and rally there.

Next they look for groups that may be able and interested in helping them get their message across and get people in the street. Given the goal of raising the minimum wage they immediately start contacting unions, as well as homeless advocacy groups to get them involved. After a bit of asking, one of the homeless organizations also recommends contacting immigrant services groups, as many of the people in this country working for minimum wage are immigrants. The students expand their contact list, and stay in touch with these groups all the way up until the march itself.

The group then starts planning timing for the day of the march. After walking the route they plan to take they find that it takes about 2½ hours to get from Red Square to Westlake Park on foot. Wanting to allow a bit of extra time to deal with slowdowns, they figure that they should give three hours for the march itself. However, they also have to allow for time to gather people before they set out, and plan for the rally afterwards, so they decide to gather at Red Square at 11, leave at noon, get to Westlake by 3, and have a few hours to rally, collect names, let people make a few speeches, and disperse by 6.

With the basic info in place they are now ready to promote their march and get the word out to the public. As they are university students they have access to copy and print shops on campus, and they draw up flyers with the march date and time, locations both for the start and end of the march (in case some people cannot make the march but want to be there for the rally afterwards) and listing the groups and organizations that are supporting this action. The students realize that by putting this information out in public they will be alerting the police and authorities to what they plan to do, but they plan to notify the police anyway and the additional public attention is deemed worth it. After printing a few hundred flyers they give a few dozen copies to each of the groups who may bring marchers (such as the unions and immigrant groups), and plaster as many as possible up in local cafes, and on sign and message boards. They also draw up a press release about the event to send to the local media, planning to e-mail them as soon as possible, and then again the day before the march. Some of the students suggest taking out advertisements in the local weeklies like *The Stranger*, but this protest is operating on a shoestring budget and they don't have the money.

As the march draws nearer, things are going smoothly and they can start collecting the gear they need for the march. Some of them are designated as march coordinators, and they make up big jackets with "Follow me!" in yellow shiny tape on the back to give the marchers a beacon to follow. A few others are set up as peacekeepers and emergency first aid, and they get white shirts with red crosses on them, as well as collecting a basic first aid kit each. In addition, each carries a few bandanas soaked in lime juice to deal with tear gas, and extra bottles of water for flushing out chemicals from marchers' eyes. This is planned to be a peaceful march, and these probably won't be needed, but it's always better to over-prepare. As for communications, each of the students has a cell phone, and a few of them go out and get bullhorns to assist with crowd control and leading chants.

At this point they also start making up signs and banners to be carried during the march. For most of the signs they just buy a few sheets of signboard and use household paints and markers to draw up signs supporting the cause, making as many extras as they can to hand out to others during the march.

In the last week before the march the first setback occurs. The city permit committee, after having said the permit would probably come through, has changed its mind. They will give a permit for the students to march, but they won't let the marchers move over the university bridge for fear of cutting off traffic for an extended period of time. As the bridge is the only real way of getting from the U-District to downtown on foot, the students can either reroute, and not go downtown, or they march without a permit. They debate turning the whole thing into a rally at Red Square and not marching at all, but they feel they would be preaching to the choir, and they want to take their message downtown. They decide to march without a permit, even with the increased risk of police and authority interference.

The day before the march itself one of the students calls each of the police precincts that the march will be passing through, introduces himself, and notifies them of when and where the march will be going. This may seem counterintuitive, especially since the permit was denied, but the cops will respond much better to protests of this type if you build a relationship with them and let them know what you are up to, and that's what the students do.

Of course the students aren't going to take anything for granted. The day of the march they enlist a friend to head up to the bridge and just wait there in case the cops do decide to cut the marchers off. If the cops move in, knowing the protesters have to use the bridge to get downtown, the friend can call the march leaders up and have them reroute as best they can to get back to Red Square and rally there. It's not what they want to do, but it beats getting completely cut off by the cops.

The students get to Red Square early, around 10:30, just in case anyone else shows up early, and set up signs, start making speeches to anyone who will listen, handing out flyers and generally making themselves visible. Over the next hour and a half people start coming in, and soon the students can look around and see about a thousand people ready to march for the cause. They had planned to start out at 12, but a few of the speeches are very good and run long, so they get going about 12:20. The point people start out, they hand out signs, and the march is finally underway. The peacekeepers follow along the sides keeping an eye out for anything that goes wrong, and the other students lead chants with the bullhorns ("1, 2, 3, 4, we support the working poor," and so on).

Calling ahead to the bridge, they find that the cops have in fact deployed a few squad cars to the area, but don't look like they are going to try to block the march. As the march gets to the bridge the coordinators try to pick up the pace a bit so that the march can get over the bridge quickly.

After winding its way a bit more through downtown the march gets to Westlake Park around 3:30, a bit later than planned but still leaving plenty of time to get their message across. They set up in Westlake Park, a downtown urban park across from the mall, and find a few dozen people there waiting to join them. The cops are also there in a bit more force, but are not trying to disrupt the rally. At this point the students and others make more speeches, pass the hat to fundraise, and pass out sign-up sheets to collect names of people interested in future protests and action.

At one point during the rally a few of the protesters start to get a bit agitated and talk about going over to the mall and breaking a few windows, but as soon as they start to walk towards the mall the peacekeepers are paying attention and stop them, threatening to call the cops over if necessary to avoid the bad press such an action would create.

The cops also get on a bullhorn to remind people that the mall itself is private property and that the protesters will be arrested if they go there. Wanting to take their message directly to some of the employers, one of the student protesters gathers a small group of people willing to get arrested and heads into the mall, sitting down in the main lobby, chanting, and refusing to move when the cops order them to. They are arrested, of course, but it takes almost an hour for the cops to draw all of them out, and the people shopping at the mall get a good view of their message.

Meanwhile, the cops outside have decided that it's time for people to go home, and around 5 they issue an order to disperse. The students had planned to stay until 6, but they feel they have gotten to make their point, they see a few television cameras in the audience so they know they'll make the news, and they don't feel a mass arrest will help their cause. One of them goes to the cops and tells them they will try to get the protest wrapped up, and the last few speeches end at 5:15. The students do a last plug to get names and contact info from people, and with a few tense waves to the cops everyone disperses and goes home, happy that the protest went well, pleased with the amount of people compelled to think about this issue, and hoping the media attention will help press government officials to vote to raise the minimum wage.

104

Of course, the protest is not over yet. The next day the students gather to go over what happened, what went well and what went poorly. Overall things went well, but of course the whole point of the protest hinges on the vote. With the contact info they gathered they can send out phone numbers for people to call their government official the day of the vote and add impact, since these are people who care enough to take action. They raised $302 in donations, which can be used to fund future protests or donated to a cause that supports low-income workers. Looking at what they should have done they discuss how people said they heard about the march and realize that they should have posted to more email and activist Web sites, as well as perhaps setting up their own Web site. With the university's resources they have everything they need to do so, and it was an oversight not to. As for the few who were arrested at the mall, they spent the night in jail, and were charged with misdemeanor trespassing and let go.

Overall the protest is a success, but if the vote doesn't go the way they want, that may require a new protest, a phone bank, or a sit-in at government offices, or...well, time to plan again.

Chapter Eleven
Stories from the Trenches:
Personal Experiences in Protests

Protests are very dynamic events, and all the planning in the world does not prepare you for the actual events on the ground. Here are some personal accounts of events at protests, told by the people who were there.

"I was at the anniversary protest of the WTO in Seattle, in a peaceful march through downtown. Several thousand marchers moved down Fourth Avenue, with all the side streets blocked off by bike cops. We were being followed by a line of cops in full riot gear (with bright orange shotguns) and were marching at a reasonable pace towards the federal building. I was towards the front of the march helping lead people, so I got to see what happened next. As the march approached Blanchard Street, another line of cops in riot gear moved in and sealed the road ahead of us. The protest organizers fell back to ask the bike cops where to go next and they were told to go north, which we could not do because of the new cops. The new cops just said they had been ordered to move in. Clearly the cops were not talking to each other, but we were left with nowhere to go. To keep everyone calm the protest organizers and peacekeepers had us all sit down in the middle of the street and wait. Well, that seemed to piss the cops right off, and some lieutenant got on a bullhorn and issued an order to disperse. This was the first order to disperse, and it was issued after we were already sealed in with nowhere to go to. Obviously we didn't move, so the cops herded us north for a bit until we were pinned between the two walls of riot gear cops, maybe 300 people trapped in 20 feet of street space. The cops issued another order to disperse, which was clearly ludicrous as we obviously had no way to leave, but the protest organizers had us all stay seated and kept anyone from getting violent. After a few minutes the cops opened one of the lines, brought in a bus and arrested everyone at the protest. We were all arrested peacefully, even though the cops were behaving illegally. For the most part we were all booked and released the next day, and the whole thing led to a nice fat lawsuit. Never fight arrest, and never argue with a cop... but always feel free to get a lawyer."

David Brown, Seattle

Of course, not all protest problems go as smoothly as a simple miscommunication and night in jail, as the next example shows.

STATEMENT OF MORGAN KATHERINE HAGER

STATE OF OREGON
County of Multinomah

I, MORGAN KATHERINE HAGER, being first duly sworn, do depose and say as follows:
    The following is a summary of what I recall about the incidents of the morning of Sunday, July 22nd and the events that followed. Even though I was injured and afraid at the time, my memories are clear (although some minor details may be inaccurate). This statement focuses on what I directly experienced or saw. When I refer to events I didn't directly experience or see, I have so indicated.
    Sherman Sparks and I, together with our friend Angeline, traveled to Genoa and participated in the peaceful protest marches there. We at no time engaged in any violence against persons or property. The G8 ended on Saturday, July 21st, and about 9 or 10 p.m. on Saturday night, Sherman and I went back to the school in Genoa where we had slept the night before. We were looking for Angeline. Angeline was not there, so I checked my e-mail and sent an e-mail to my parents, telling them that everything was fine, the protests had ended, we were safe, and we were going to leave Genoa first thing the next morning. We considered joining Angeline, who was sleeping at another location (one of many camps in and around Genoa), but by this time we were too tired to find another place to sleep. Anyway, we thought the school would be the safest

place to sleep. The camps didn't seem to be safe because we had been told the police had visited them on a number of occasions and the encounters were not pleasant, although not violent. Also, the school was across the street from the Indy Media Center that housed the media, took care of the injured, etc., so we perceived that the closeness gave the school some protection.

Sherman and I lay down in our sleeping bags on the first floor at about 11:00 p.m. We fell asleep. I can't remember if Sherman woke me, or if I woke because of all the noise. Regardless, I woke to crashing and yelling outside. There was chaos everywhere. People were running around trying to collect their belongings. There was a great deal of noise: The police were breaking down the doors and smashing the windows. I later heard that someone had barricaded the doors after the trouble started out in the street and at the media center. I quickly began collecting my belongings, but I didn't manage to get my shoes on or collect my belongings before the police entered the room.

Sherman and I were sleeping behind a wall so we did not have a view of the main entrance to the school. Across the room, the people sleeping there had a direct view of the entry. The first thing I noticed was that the people across the room, which was the largest group of people in the room (there were many more scattered throughout the room), were getting down on their knees and putting their hands up in signs of peace or non-resistance/surrender. All of those across the room, about 15 in total, were doing that. Sherman and I immediately did the same thing.

The police rushed into the room. They were dressed in dark clothing, and may have had protective vests, etc., under their clothing because they looked exceedingly bulky. They wore helmets with plastic face covers (riot helmets, I think). They wore heavy boots, gloves, and carried batons (clubs). I am certain no skin was showing on any of them. I later learned that these police were part of an anti-terrorist force called the DIGOS. I know the Italian press has reported that 20 policemen were hospitalized after the raid on the school, but that is difficult to believe based on what I saw and experienced.

The first thing I recall the police doing was kicking a chair into the group of people kneeling on the floor. I could hear things smashing this whole time. A few police (5 or 7 or so) ran into the room. One came over to our corner and, as I was kneeling with my hands extended, he kicked me in the side of the head, knocking me to the floor. Sherman and another man who had been sleeping near us helped me back up to my knees. Another policeman came to where I was kneeling and started beating me with his club. I was up against the wall, and I curled over with my right side against the wall and my hands and arms covering my head for protection. I tried not to move because I thought he would stop beating me sooner if I lay still. I am not sure how many policemen were beating me. I looked up and saw Sherman being beaten. After they stopped beating us, Sherman and I lay curled up by the wall for about five minutes or so. I think at this point the police were bringing people down from the upper two floors.

I noticed that there was a lot of blood around us, and that blood was smeared on the wall. I think it was our blood because we were both bleeding from the head, and I was bleeding from my hands and wrists. About 5 minutes later, the police ordered everyone in the room to go over against the opposite wall. As I was walking across the room to do so, the policeman who told us to move struck me in the butt with his club. We all curled up against the opposite wall. At this point I noticed that my bleeding right hand was swollen, and my little finger was sticking out at a strange angle. Sherman's eyes looked glazed and he wasn't responding to questions normally.

We sat against the wall as more people were herded into the room and basically piled up with us against the wall. All had been beaten, and some had to be carried down the stairs by others who had also been beaten. I was shaking and couldn't stop. We stayed against the wall for 5 or 10 minutes more until paramedics in orange suits started arriving. (I was told later that they were volunteers — not working for the government.) By the time the paramedics started arriving, the original policemen who had done the beatings were gone and the room was full of different police wearing the Carabinieri uniforms (basically riot police)."

110

Raises the hair on the back of your neck, doesn't it? Examples like this show the great importance of protesters looking out for one another. Anything can happen out there.

Of course, not all protests are done by individuals. The USA Patriot act inspired many protests across the country, and will surely inspire more as it is implemented, but perhaps none of those protests are as inspiring as a simple resolution passed by the Benton County, Oregon, County Commissioners. If things get really bad, look for me in Benton.

The resolution, D2003-111, passed by the County Commissioners says:

"Resolution:

Whereas, several actions recently taken by the federal government, including the adoption of the 'Uniting and Strengthening America by Providing Appropriate Tools Required to Intercept and Obstruct Terrorism Act,' also known as the USA Patriot Act, several Executive Orders, and the 'Homeland Security Act,' may cause the federal government to violate the following when pursuing matters of security:

Freedom of speech, assembly and privacy;

Fundamental liberties protected by due process and probable cause;

The right to legal counsel in judicial proceedings; and

Protection from unreasonable searches and seizures; all of which are guaranteed to all residents of the United States by the Constitutions of Oregon and the United States; and whereas, there is conflicting federal legislation that directly impacts the ability of Benton County employees to respond to requests for assistance and access to personal and confidential information;

Therefore, be it resolved that the Benton County Board of Commissioners, hereby:

1. Directs county employees to direct requests, including court orders, warrants and subpoenas from federal authorities under the aforementioned federal legislation or directives to the

highest supervisory level: the sheriff for law enforcement and the Board of Commissioners for all others;

    2. Directs all county departments to continue their strong commitment to preserve residents' freedom of speech, religion, assembly and privacy; and;

    3. Urges local law enforcement entities to continue to be vigilant in preserving the rights of the people of Benton County as guaranteed by the Oregon and United States Constitutions.

    Be it further resolved that the Benton County Board of Commissioners requests that our United States representatives and senators monitor the implementation of federal legislation and executive directives and actively work to correct or repeal those parts of such legislation that violate our rights and liberties as stated in the Constitution of the United States.

    Therefore, in recognition that residents of Benton County, Oregon, are a diverse population and include non-citizens whose contributions to the community are vital to its character and function, the Benton County Board of Commissioners asserts its commitment to defend the constitutionally protected rights to liberty, justice and the pursuit of happiness from unnecessary government intrusion."

Protests are very dynamic events, and many things can go wrong. I cannot stress enough the importance of doing your homework and making sure you have all your facts correct. As a final example of what can go wrong, consider Jody Mason of Olympia, Washington. Jody wanted to lock himself to a federal Department of Energy office building to protest "President" Bush's energy policy. This is classic direct action, a very good way to get media attention, and if you are willing to accept the risks is a very good method of protest, but only if you get the right building. That's right, at 11 in the morning Jody successfully locked himself to the State Grange office building. The cops came by eventually and cut him out and let him go. This could have been a very strong message against the government's energy policy, and instead it became such a

112

joke the cops didn't even arrest him. Lesson: Do your homework.

Chapter Twelve
Advanced Tips and Tricks:
Strategy and Tactics
for Protest Success,
and Scarier Ways
You Can Be Fucked With

114

There are hundreds of things you can do to help ensure that your protest gets the results you want. In addition to planning your main protest (a march, a picket line, and so on) you can dramatically increase your impact by using some of these tactics. Here are some advanced tricks that can be used on their own or with other types of protests to help you communicate your message and get results.

"Haunting" Public Officials

One point to protests is to get in the face of your target and get your point to them directly. A politician who might ignore your letter will have trouble ignoring you if he has to walk past a picket line outside his office building. "Haunting" takes that idea one step further, with one person or a small team follows them everywhere they go. When they come to work, you are there. When they go to a meeting, you are there. When they go out for coffee, meet others for lunch, or go home for the day, you are there. This is almost guaranteed to get them riled, but if they cannot go about their day without constantly seeing your message, you can insure you have impact on their decision-making.

This tactic can require quite a few people, as the first response is often to arrest the protesters, and you will need to replace people as they are arrested. This can actually increase your impact, as the target keeps seeing new faces and new people, but always holding the same sign and delivering the same message.

Public Art/Graffiti

People holding signs are transient, but spray paint is forever (or at least much harder to remove). If you have some artistic skills and chutzpa you may be able to make your message clear in new ways with a paintbrush. The opportunities are legion. Protesting police brutality? Spray paint, "Warning Citizens, Police in Area," and watch the cops turn red. Angry that roads never get maintained? A few quick brushstrokes turn every street sign into "Pot Hole Rd." And, of course, a new statue in city hall (bought with taxpayer money better used elsewhere) is just dying to be "improved."

This tactic is almost always fun, but also almost always illegal. However, even if you are trying to stay out of jail you can use this. Look for ways to put art in the public eye legally. Does a local shop have an exterior wall you could paint a mural on? Could local community members tape art pieces to the sides of their cars? Keep your eyes and mind open and you can find all kinds of places to put art. The added bonus for staying legal is that it makes it much harder for your target to fight back. Spray paint can be painted over, but the cops can't (legally) do much about what people choose to display themselves.

Sympathetic Symbols/Buttons/Ribbons

Not everyone will be deeply involved and committed to your protest, but many will be quietly supportive of your cause. You can use this to your advantage by giving them a way to show support for your cause. It seems these days that every cause has a colored ribbon (those wanting to show support for a variety of causes could easily look like a rainbow) but you can use almost anything, ribbons, buttons, even paperclips have been used to voice quiet support for the cause. This serves your cause in several ways, both by raising public awareness ("Hey, why am I the only person without a yellow button?") and by showing your target that you have broad support ("Hey, look at all the customers with yellow buttons. Maybe I have to take these people seriously.").

Tax/Fee Refusal

In some cases you can add economic impact to your protests by refusing to pay taxes or fees that support activities you don't believe in. People have refused to pay a portion of their taxes to the U.S. government in protest of wars and the military-industrial complex (or refused to pay tax at all because of the difficulty to sort out which money goes where). Any time a fee or tax is levied there is the potential for a protest of this sort. A library that won't carry "banned" books (like *Hamlet*, *The Origin of Species*, even *Civil Disobedience*) could find that no one is paying their late fees. A city that passes transportation policies people don't like may find no one paying their car licensing fees. Especially when dealing with the government, this tends to be illegal, but when you are impacting people's pocketbooks as well as their eyes you may find you get action (for or against you) faster.

Building/Facility Overloading

Sometimes rather than protesting a business or area by walking away, the best route is to protest by showing up in droves. Unlike a sit-in, here the idea is to be a legitimate user of the service, but in such a way that you make it impossible for the business to stay functioning. If a major supermarket is fighting a union action you might bring hundreds of people to line up and buy 10¢ sticks of chewing gum over and over, bringing their real grocery sales to a standstill. A university that is refusing to allow students to publish an independent newspaper could have their office functionally closed by waves of students all requesting copies of the same form.

This can be used even if there is no building to fill. In protest of the required registration with the Selective Service System, during the Vietnam War many people chose to take the legal requirement of notifying the government when they changed status literally, flooding the government offices with letters filled with information the government didn't want. From registering even when they were too old to be drafted, to going as far as mailing a letter saying they were moving to Europe in three weeks, followed in a week with a new letter saying they've changed their minds, people swamped the government offices with irrelevant mail that they were compelled to process anyway. Every hour that the government spent reading these letters was another hour that they were not finding young men to draft.

Mass Prayer

Religion is a very deeply ingrained element of almost every society, and mass prayers have been used throughout time to show collective will and solidarity. In addition, mass prayer can make your target far less willing to hassle you, and can have a protective quality. A line of protesters yelling at cops may make a tempting target for aggressive police action, but a line of protesters kneeling in prayer are much less likely to be treated roughly.

It is important also to think of the protesters you will be working with. Some ecology-minded Christian protesters attending "Save the Earth"-type events have been alienated by the heavy pagan atmosphere. Try to avoid casting aside allies when going this route.

Some protests (such as the ongoing cloning debate) may lend themselves more strongly to a prayer element than others, and you want to avoid alienating potential allies who may not share your religion, but prayer can be used effectively as a nonviolent tool to aid your protest.

Mock Awards

Mock awards serve as a great way to have fun pointing out the evils and missteps of your target, and can be more effective than other, more blatantly hostile protests. Using humor to get your point across tends to make good press, and this can serve as a good add-on to other protests to help keep your issue on the front page of the newspapers.

The basic idea of the mock award is to "award" your target a prize, trophy, or other award to draw attention to how they are acting. A company opening a new sweatshop in the Third World to avoid American wages and laws might be awarded a giant check for 27¢ to cover the first hour of the first worker's pay. A university administrator who cuts funding to a student paper might be awarded the first copy of the new paper (written on an index card). Any good visual works well, but the most important thing for mock awards is media coverage. If you make your target look foolish, but no one is watching, you have no effect. Do this on camera and it can be quite effective.

Skywriting/Large-scale Writing

One sure way to get your message across is to think big. This is basically the tactic of writing a large message where many people will see it, and in such a way that it is very difficult to move or hide. Using a plane to skywrite "Ban the Bomb" over a nuclear processing plant, or arranging white rocks on a dark field to spell out anti-war slogans that can be read by planes taking off from a nearby air force base, or painting anti-globalization messages high up on the sides of buildings that will be visible from the conference rooms of world economic leaders, all force people to at least see your message. It can be difficult to put such a large message in place, but if you think big enough you can put up messages that are very difficult to take back down.

Guerrilla Theatre

One of the best ways to get your message into people's minds is to involve them directly, get them into the loop whether they want to be or not. Guerrilla theatre includes everything from the street plays being done in Africa to raise AIDS awareness to more invasive tactics, including such quasi-legal actions as those of the group that spent a few hours on the streets of New York ordering people up against the wall, asking for ID and asking personal questions, all without identifying themselves, just to see how few people would ask who they were or assert their rights.

This takes a lot of planning, and often takes a lot of guts, but it can be a good way to get your message right into people's minds. Planning is paramount, and you have to script out what you want to happen and what you are going to do. If you just want to do a short skit on the roadside as people pass, this can be a good addition to other protests. Getting more elaborate, and more invasive, this can be a protest unto itself. When used as a tactic to disrupt an existing event (such as crashing a news conference on water quality by drinking a glass of tap water and gagging and choking) this can be the best way available to make your point.

Perhaps the most important point to be made with theatre is to remember that your audience may not have much background on your issue. You want to ensure that your audience does not stand around saying, "What are they talking about?" So don't get too esoteric. Try presenting your piece to friends who are not familiar with your issue first. If they don't get it, odds are the public won't.

Police Distraction

Almost any protest is going to draw police, and in many cases you know ahead of time that you are likely to receive an unenthusiastic welcome by the local cops. By planning accordingly you can work to reduce the police's ability to interfere with your main protest. If you want to stage a march without a permit and worry about getting cut off you might start a false march with a few large banners to draw the cops' attention elsewhere while you get your real march started. A small team of people might link hands and block the cops (until they get arrested) from moving in a certain area as you set up signs or displays. You can even get more deceptive if you know the authorities are doing things like monitoring your walkie talkies (easy to do) by calling out that you are doing one thing on the radio (such as setting up at a faraway park) when really doing something different. This requires having good communications on the ground, but the joy of watching the cops run in circles is worth it.

Morale Boosters

Any protest that runs long, such as a long-term picket line, can wear on your protesters. In order to keep morale up and attract public attention to your cause you may want to add morale boosters to your protest. Have a large picnic (maybe right next to, or even in the road you are picketing next to). Call in a masseuse (finding one sympathetic to your cause may even get you a discount). Hire a clown and have a party for all the protesters' kids. Whatever it takes to keep long-term protesters involved and keep morale up. For any long-term, large-scale protest this can be a huge help.

Jail Solidarity

One downside to large-scale public protests is the risk that a large number of protesters will be arrested. For some protests you can use the sheer number of people being picked up by the police as a tool to further voice your displeasure with the system while at the same time both making things difficult for the authorities and, in some cases, avoiding jail altogether.

The police may have authority in jails, but that authority derives from people's willingness to follow their orders. If ahead of time (and this sort of tactic must be planned well in advance) you and your fellow protesters decide on mass non-cooperation, a complete refusal to comply with police demands, then you can grind the system to a halt. If the cops want to process 60 people, people who won't give their names, won't make it easy to fingerprint them, won't even move unless they are picked up and carried, they may (and have in the past) simply let everyone go, or offer a minor charge such as a traffic ticket, rather than go to the extreme effort needed to process so many non-cooperating persons.

In order for this to work it is critical that you and your fellow protesters are not carrying any ID or other identifying documents the cops can (and will) seize and use to ID you. For calls to your lawyers or other persons, you should use prearranged code names, with the lawyer having a master sheet to cross-reference and determine who has been arrested. Jail solidarity takes a lot of planning, and can be risky, but can allow you to use your mass of numbers as a weapon the police cannot defend against.

Carried further, even if you do wind up in jail you can use your numbers as a weapon again, insisting on individual jury trials, not waiving any hearings, and using every legal trick you can to take the most court time possible. Courts are so overtaxed now that in some cases the government has decided to simply release protesters rather than fill the courts with endless low-level trials.

Strike Alternatives

Strikes can be costly and risky. Here are a few tactics that are alternatives to conventional strikes.

Working to the letter of contracts: One way to protest working conditions, low pay and other workplace problems is to do only the job you are paid to do. Instead of walking out or striking, the workers do their jobs, and only their jobs. One example would be teachers in public high schools (who might want to avoid the negative press a full strike might bring) refusing to do extra-curricular work, not staying late to supervise student activities, not writing letters of recommendation, basically not doing anything other than what is specified in their contracts. Most modern high schools would be unable to function without the extra unpaid work put in by teachers, and such a protest is guaranteed to draw attention.

Work slowdowns: Modern corporate America lives or dies on the productivity of its workers. This empowers workers to express their displeasure by working below their most productive, to introduce inefficiencies to the workplace, and in general to slow things down. Done properly it can be hard to blame any one worker, but the impact on the bottom line demands attention.

The exact method of slowing things down will be different in each case, from slowing an assembly line to insuring that needed parts are never in stock, but a deep look at how your workplace operates should show several areas where things can be gummed up. For those willing to be slightly less legal, low-level sabotage is an option. Even having the office copier go down due to a "leaky" ink cartridge can slow work to a crawl.

Reverse strikes: Most people view strikes as people walking off the job; in a reverse strike the idea is to stay on the job, stay at work, but work for your own ends. This in many cases can actually have a greater financial impact on your target because facilities stay open, raw materials and equipment get used, but no profit comes in. A newspaper could stay open, reporting on issues the workers feel are important, and run the presses to print papers with no advertising, intending to distribute the papers to increase public awareness and sympathy for the workers. In addition to the loss of advertising revenue, the company also has the material costs for paper, ink, machine wear and tear and so on.

124

This relatively new tactic has been used by coal miners, staying at the mine but selling the coal themselves, and the potential is there for this to be used more extensively as it proves to be effective.

Quickie/lightning strikes: In many cases workers may want to avoid a full-scale strike, or in some cases (such as the police force) may be legally and socially unable to strike, but want to make their displeasure and unity clear to their employers. The lightning strike provides a way for workers to make a point without the costs and risks of a full strike. In a lightning strike employees strike for a small duration, perhaps ten minutes, rising out of their chairs in unison and walking out. The idea isn't to cause economic cost but to show employers that the workers are serious, have concerns and need to be dealt with. The sight of an office empty in the middle of the day, even for a few minutes, may be enough to scare employers to the bargaining table.

Detailed/layered strikes: Another way to show your displeasure without the difficulties and cost of a full strike is a layered strike, a strike in which employees protest by division. For example, in a bottling plant the equipment maintenance personnel might strike first, then a few days later the people who drive the trucks, then the low-level managers, and so on. This allows the employer to watch as more and more of the work staff walks and the factory empties, encouraging them to act quickly to avoid any loss of revenue. This could also be structured such that one worker goes on strike each day, slowly emptying offices.

This style of strike has the advantage of letting workers who may be less able to financially survive being out of work for long to support the strike by being one of the later people to strike, letting people with more savings walk first. In addition, if a few key divisions strike and shut down a company, other workers in divisions that are supportive but not officially striking may be able to draw unemployment. Having even a little money coming in can help keep people going while a strike works itself out.

Turning Tricks

Of course your target has tools available to try to shut you up, keep you in line, and shut you down. You should not let the possibility of retribution quench your fires, but it is important to understand what can happen in response to your protests. In addition to arrest, fines, and other risks (see the chapter on risk assessment) here are some of the advanced tactics that can be used against you.

Counter protests: This is a very common tactic, especially if your protests have been well publicized. If you want to stand in the streets holding signs, others may choose to stand across the street and hold signs saying you are wrong. This is actually a good thing, and can work for you if you play it correctly, as conflict like this should draw more media attention. Your big concerns should be to avoid (or at least not start) violence, as tempers can run high with protesters for different sides in such close proximity. In addition, try to out-protest your opposition, with more people, bigger signs, and so on. Conflict like this is the basis of any democracy, but if you can't sit across the table and talk, at least try to be the one shouting the loudest.

On the subject of shouting the loudest, the main problem of counter protests may be that of dealing with the media. The media is your main tool for talking to the public, but in the case of counter protests the media may often fall into the "equal coverage" trap, telling the public each side's opinion with equal force even if the number of protesters is radically different. Showing up with a thousand people and watching someone with a few dozen get equal coverage is aggravating. Try keeping your signs in front of (or at least somewhere visible behind) theirs, and keep them surrounded by your people to prevent the media from getting a crowd shot that makes it look like they have a large number of supporters.

Protest infiltration: The less democratic and more insidious flipside of counter protests, here your target (or others) attempts to infiltrate your protest and shut it down or hurt your effectiveness. By being on the "inside" your target gains advanced knowledge of your actions, and can counter many of them. If they know you plan to crash a board meeting they can reschedule, shutting you down before you even start. This has also, legal or not, been used historically by governments to infiltrate "subversive" groups and keep tabs on citizens unwilling to toe the party line. This is used especially to track and locate groups who are acting illegally. If you plan to engage in any even quasi-legal activities it cannot be stressed enough that you should not be working with anyone you do not trust completely. Consult *Ecodefense: A Field Guide to Monkeywrenching* for a good look at some of the security measures you should take to protect yourself and your actions.

A variant of this tactic is protest funding, giving money or other support to protesters through third parties. While you may find the money useful, having the public discover the source of your funding can kill your credibility. Protesting a chemical plant on environmental grounds is noble, but if the media reports that you got tons of money from companies that compete with your target in producing chemicals you wind up looking like a corporate tool.

You can help to protect yourself from this by operating only in affinity groups, groups of trusted friends and allies that you know ahead of time. Most major protests today are maintained by coalitions of affinity groups.

Beyond being hyperparanoid there isn't much you can do to avoid the powers that be keeping tabs on your actions. Keeping the harsh light of the media on you can help to ensure the authorities can't get too far out of line, but for the most part you just have to be aware that even among your own group you may not all always be working for the same goal.

Protest deflection: Wise PR people, when faced with active protesters, will take action to keep you out of the public view and off the evening news. From offering to let picketers come in out of the rain to trying to get all the protest organizers to come in for a meeting (and thus stop leading the protesters), to just shutting a building down and cutting the lights and power, your target may try just about anything to corral you. This can cut your effectiveness quite a bit, and may have the added benefit for them of letting them appear friendly and cooperative while shutting you down.

You need to have this possibility in mind when dealing with offers from your target, and while negotiation and cooperation are never out of the question, make sure you still have a position to argue from when you sit down at the negotiating table.

Giving in without following up: When you are standing in the company lobby chanting, your target may say just about anything to get you to shut up and go away, even if it means agreeing with your demands. The risk is that once you go away they will put you out of their minds and not follow up with their commitments. This is a very common response to protests, and whenever you get people to agree to your request you should have a timeline of what will happen when. The best way to keep your target in line is usually to get their agreement in writing. Even a quickly jotted down list of agreements, signed and dated, will have the effect of keeping them honest. Such a document may have no legal standing, but the act of signing it will embed the agreement in their mind and give you a tool to show the media if they back down. Then, after the protest you need to stay in contact with your target to remind them to stay on course, and that you are watching them. Of course, if they don't comply with your requests and follow up on their commitments you may just have to protest again.

Lawsuits: In our increasingly litigious society it should come as no surprise that the big corporations (with their huge legal teams) will be quite willing to sue you to shut you up. Cases can be brought for defamation of character, slander, libel, and as many other issues as they can think of to tack on. There is even a term for lawsuits brought for the sole purpose of shutting people up: SLAPP lawsuits (Strategic Lawsuits Against Public Participation). Even in cases where the company knows it has no case it may sue anyway, knowing that the cost and hassle of defending against a lawsuit may be enough to shut you up. They may even sue, and then agree to settle out of court if you'll agree to shut up, an offer that can look good when you have a multimillion-dollar lawsuit hanging over your head.

In some areas, laws are being changed to allow protesters working for the public interest to get these cases thrown out quickly, but you (and your lawyer) should be aware that these lawsuits can take quite a lot of time and energy, energy that you then cannot use to continue your protests.

On the upside, one response you may be able to use is to countersue your target. If you can prove that they were suing you purely in the interest of getting you to shut up you may be able to win damages that not only will cover your legal fees, but may also include additional awards to discourage companies from using lawsuits as a gag for protesters.

What Has Come Before:
Protests in History

Protest deflection in action: In 1966 several hundred protesters arrived at a U.S. Air Force base to protest a recent decision not to use some of the unused areas of the base property for low-income housing. Faced with hundreds of protesters on his doorstep, some quick thinking officer came out, spoke with the protesters, and offered them a tour of the base. The protesters accepted, loaded into Air Force busses and were given a tour, shown around and most importantly kept off the evening news. By taking the protesters out of the public view the Air Force was able to render the protest irrelevant, and by doing it in a peaceful and even friendly way they got to look like the good guys for doing so.

Chapter Thirteen
Tools of the Trade:
How to Build Your Protest
Survival Pack

You can go out and protest with nothing more than a good pair of shoes and a loud voice, but if you plan your protest in advance and you pack accordingly you can have dramatically more impact.

Your protest pack (which could be an actual backpack, a shoulder bag, or whatever works) is intended to get you through the protest, keep you on your feet and energized, and provide the tools to enhance your protest's effectiveness. As protest organizers you want to make sure everything goes as well as possible at your protest, and paying attention to your kits will help keep you at peak effectiveness.

Even if you aren't planning a protest right now, you can create a pack in preparation for a protest, ensuring that when the time comes to take to the streets you are ready to go.

What you need to have in your pack is determined by many factors, but the key factor is weight (you may have to carry this around for many hours). Some items (marked with a *) probably do not need to be carried by every protest organizer, but you want to make sure there is at least one present and easily available. Here are some ideas for what to include for protests of differing time commitments.

Short-term Protests

For short-term protests which last from a few hours to one day, such as a march, you will need:

Food:

An *energy bar* for every two hours you expect to be protesting (at least three bars).

Bottled water or other fluid. (Avoid coffee, soda or other dehydrating fluid.) Try to have at least 12 ounces of water every few hours.

For protests of more than eight hours you may want to pack a sandwich, some dried fruit or other light snack. Pack any food items in easily carried, watertight containers.

Tools:

Pens and paper. Every protest organizer should carry a small pad of paper and a few pens and pencils in order to write down notes, get contact information, record events and so on.

Simple medical kit*. You don't need a full medical kit, but having Band-Aids and aspirin on hand can keep you on your feet longer.

Cell phones or walkie talkies*. It is very helpful if all of your protest organizers have a way to contact each other as the protest goes on.

Extra batteries. Everyone with a cell phone or walkie talkie should have at least one extra battery. Assume you will be unable to recharge your equipment for the duration of the protest and pack accordingly.

Large black markers. For making last minute signs.

Bright tape*. For marking arrows or notes on the ground or walls as needed, mostly important for mobile protests like marches. For those willing to break more laws you could also go with spray paint, which is harder to remove.

Duct tape*. Almost anything can be fixed with duct tape.

Personal information:

Identification. Even in the least confrontational protest you always run the risk of running into trouble and winding up in jail. Unless your group has agreed ahead of time to avoid any cooperation with the police make sure you have your ID handy.

The phone number of your lawyer. This should often be written in indelible ink on your arm, just in case you get separated from your belongings at the police station. Again, even if you don't plan to need it, have it.

134

Business cards. If you have time, print up cards with your name, phone number and e-mail address on them to pass out to people you meet so you can network and possibly work together again in the future. This can also be helpful if you need to pass your contact information out to witnesses of something about which you may need their testimony in court.

Emergency equipment:

Gas mask/damp cloth. Remember that the cops are unlikely to respond well to visible gas masks, and no one without proper training should use them.

Video camera/Still camera*. Even a cheap disposable camera (which you can pick up at any major store) may be helpful for documentation. As has been mentioned before, the cops may be less likely to step out of line if on camera. Remember two things, first that anything you photograph may show up in court, so you have to watch what you do as well, and that cops carry clubs for a reason, so don't bring the thousand dollar video camera if you can't bear the thought of it getting smashed up.

Police band scanner. This is not needed for protests with permits, and may not be needed unless you plan a mobile, aggressive protest such as a snake march, but having one person with a cell phone listening to police band radio can alert you when their plans change.

Medium-term Protests

For medium-term protests lasting a few days, such as a sit-in, you will need all the items listed above, plus:

Personal items:

Toiletries. Toothbrush, toothpaste, perhaps breath mints or two. Toilet paper is a must, even if you don't expect to need it.

Additional food. You may be able to have food brought in from the outside, but assume you are on your own and pack accordingly.

Clothing. Depending on your protest you will need extra clothing from just a new shirt to wet weather gear, a warm coat, or suntan lotion.

Bedding. A warm coat and a backpack may serve as bedding, but if you can pack a small pillow and blanket, do so.

Repair/backup tools:

Extra signs, tape, and so on to repair signs and protest materials that break down over the course of the protest.

Extra film. If you are carrying a camera make sure you have enough film to shoot without worrying about running out.

Equipment:

Radio. You want to be able to keep up on how your protest is being reported in the media, and possibly modify your protest accordingly. If you have a small portable television you might also bring that.

Long-term Protests

For long-term protests that last more than a few days, such as a tree sitting, you will need all the above items, plus:

Personal items:

Additional food. Again, you should plan to be self-contained and carry as much of your own food and water as you can.

Entertainment. You are almost certain to have periods of down time when you have no camera or passersby to yell slogans at. A good book (especially one that will keep you focused on your reason for protesting) is good for filling the slow times. And, of course, you can always carry *this* book.

Cell phone. In shorter-term protests you may want a cell phone, in a long-term protest it is a must. You will have long periods of time when the media and the public are looking elsewhere, and if something important occurs (such as the cops moving in) you want to have your local media on speed dial.

What Has Come Before:
Protests in History

Some protesters choose a more direct route for their protests. Eco-warriors (ecological sabotage specialists) have done everything from spiking trees and roads to "relocating" equipment to even less legal actions in defense of what they feel is right.

In 1985, in Hawaii, a team of such eco-warriors were concerned about deforestation of the islands' rainforests, and dealt with it by firebombing a $250,000 wood chipper. The loss of such an expensive and hard to replace piece of equipment drove the company in question out of business, and slowed deforestation for years.

Chapter Fourteen
Getting Your Act Together:
Working With a Group
or Starting Your Own

Protests tend to be very labor intensive, and if you want to have impact you need a good group of people to work with. From phone trees, to getting permits, to writing signs, to getting people out of jail, if you try to do everything yourself you are going to burn out before you even get off the ground. In order to find the allies you need to work for your cause you have two choices: Join an existing group with similar goals, or form your own group. Both options can provide you the people and resources you need, but each option has downsides.

Joining an Existing Group

There are hundreds of thousands of organizations working towards changing the world for the better. From worldwide non-governmental organizations like Amnesty International to your local PTA, you can always find people to work with. By joining up with an existing group you gain quite a few benefits:

Existing resources: Any large organization needs a certain amount of basic infrastructure in order to function. By joining a group that already has that infrastructure in place you can use it, without the need to create it yourself. Some groups will just let you use their faxes and phones, some will cut you a check to help fund events, and most actively want to help protests related to their causes.

Political clout/name recognition: Many groups have spent long years establishing a reputation and a history of success. If you start a group dedicated to protecting the environment you may have to explain your goals, your methods, and your hopes. If you can say, "I'm with Greenpeace," most people will immediately get the idea.

Personnel: Many groups, especially groups with a national or international scope, have a large following and can provide hands and feet for your protest. This can also be useful for networking if you need resources beyond your local area. Want to fly to D.C. to picket the White House? It helps to have a group that can help you find someone to stay with (assuming the cops don't take care of lodging for you). You may meet some great friends you wind up working with for years.

Of course many of the elements of a large organization may work at cross-purposes to your goals. Some things to think about:

Existing agendas/tactics: Groups that have been around for years build up not only a main goal, but many existing opinions and agendas related to their main issues. Some of these agendas may not be things you are comfortable with. Continuing the Greenpeace example, if you want to work within a government system to help pass laws to protect salmon, you may not want to be associated in politicians' minds with people blockading fishing boats and standing in front of harpoons.

Size/timeliness: As groups get larger they become slower, needing more time to move information and ideas around and taking more time to act. While working with an existing group may add dozens of people to help you, if you want to be in the streets tomorrow you may not want to wait for the larger group to catch up to you.

Forming Your Own Group

By choosing instead to start your own group you have different issues to worry about. Some of the benefits:

Speed: Since you don't have to answer to anybody you can act as you see fit, and get moving faster than might otherwise be the case.

Local flavor: By being a local group you may be seen as more credible on a local issue. A national organization opposing a logging company may be vulnerable to charges of trying to destroy the logging industry, but a local group is just protecting its community.

140

Freedom of action: When you are acting on your own the only people you have to answer to is yourself. You don't have to deal with a national organization concerned with how its logo is used, how its name is used, or how you represent them. The time you would spend complying with those rules can be used acting.

Of course these benefits are a tradeoff, and there are many difficulties you have to overcome when working on your own.

Infrastructure/resources: Without existing structure to work with, you have to create the whole group from scratch. Time and money you spend building up that structure takes energy that could be used more directly changing things.

Personnel: If you are working on your own, you have to use your own people to handle everything. This lack of hands can sometimes limit the scope of what you can do.

Credibility: Without the backing of a larger parent organization it may be easier for your opponents to dismiss you as irrelevant, as just a bunch of local nuts. You can overcome this opinion with well run protests and well thought out debate, but you will have to make a name for yourself.

Overall you have to decide for yourself if you want to join up with an existing group or start your own. If you need to act quickly, if your issue is more local, or if you want more freedom of action you may want to get a group together yourself. If you need the resources, people and clout of an existing organization, get on the phone and sign up.

What Has Come Before:
Protests in History

The Industrial Workers of the World has a long history of fighting for workers' rights and the needs of the common worker. Founded in 1905, they received their first real national attention in 1912, when they aided a strike of textile workers in Lawrence, Massachusetts. The strikers went to the picket line, marched through local stores, held sit-ins in the street when ordered to disperse by police, and defied both the local police and the militia.

One particular tactic that proved effective, if costly, was to bring the strikers' children and child laborers to the picket line. Police, in an inexcusable moment of folly, beat the children with clubs, and the resultant publicity (eventually including a congressional investigation) forced the hand of the strikers' opponents and led to a settlement.

Chapter Fifteen
Alternatives to Protest

It is important to remember that taking to the streets is only one way to get what you want. Active protests can create change, but you may be able to get what you want in other ways as well, and in many cases protests are most effective as part of a larger strategy to create change.

Here are some other things to do when you are trying to change the system.

144

Lawsuits

Large corporations and local governments may not respond to a bunch of long-haired freaks with signs on the doorstep, but they will pay attention rather quickly to a lawyer and a subpoena.

In order to go this route you need to do both a lot of homework and a lot of legwork. First you need to find a lawyer who will work with you and help the fight for your cause. Lawyers aren't cheap, but if you look hard enough you can often find a good ally. If you are fighting a company that's dumping toxins in the water you may be able to find a lawyer living downstream who will be quite willing to join your cause. Work ahead of time if you can to cultivate good lawyers, build your relationship with them, and you can rely on them to do what they can for you when the handcuffs go on.

Once you find a lawyer who will help, it is time to do your homework and make sure you know the laws in question. Ideally your lawyers will assist, and their skilled eyes will be critical, but you need to know for yourself what is impacting your argument.

Lawsuits are not quick, but can be more effective than years of protest. Companies can be compelled by the courts to clean up their acts, and large cash awards can both give you the resources to continue your fight and serve as a warning to other companies to keep their noses clean as well. Just receiving a letter on nice legal letterhead, written in a firm, polite, demanding tone can often be enough to bring your opposition over to your way of seeing things.

It is also worth noting that there is nothing that says you can only do one or the other. For example, if your company violates its contract with the workers you may want to go on strike while also bringing in lawyers and suing for breach of contract. Keeping pressure on from all sides can be more effective than any single attempt to change behavior.

Public Office

One popular target for protests is the government, that great, bloated bureaucracy that passes all those crazy laws and serves the needs of special interests. Government is particularly well-suited as a target for protests (after all they are supposed to represent public opinion and need) and the openness of government, with its public hearings and open meeting laws, makes it easier both to get information and get in front of the people with the authority to make changes.

But if they are slow to change, if they aren't responding to your needs, why not be the people making the changes yourself? Dislike how the city council votes? Hate the mayor's new policies? Consider running for office yourself. If you are angry enough about what your local government is doing, and if enough of the public agrees with you, you have a platform you may be able to use to get yourself in office.

The Media

One key element of every protest should be trying to get the best coverage you can in the media. Most of the public won't see you on the picket line in person, they won't hear your cries in the streets. What they form their opinion from will be the 30-second blurb on the nightly news and the short article written in the local paper. Therefore, you want to make sure you get the best coverage you can, and what better way to do that than to be the media yourself.

It takes a great deal of work to make a full newspaper (and still more to do a video press release), but with some simple software and a few hours you can put out a newsletter and get your information and opinions directly into the public view. Publish regularly and provide useful information and you may create more change than with weeks of marches.

The Internet has been a boon for many elements of culture, but in few places has it been as useful as for getting protesters around the world onto the same page, combining their desire and drive for a better world into one coherent force, working as one mind to change the world. One of the best examples of this can be found at www.indymedia.org, the Independent Media Center, a group that is one of the best places to find information on protests of all kinds, affecting every citizen of the world. Many protests benefit from building their own Web site, and this is a prime example of how to do it right.

For-Profit Corporations

Many problems have solutions that not only help the world, but also make money. Recycling companies may help the planet, but they also pay salaries. Protesting companies that test soap on animals? Why not start a company that sells organic, no-animal-testing soap. (The Body Shop was founded on this idea, and does quite well.) This may prove to be quite a lot more effort than a protest, but it can be much more satisfying to provide the public an option and put your target out of business economically.

What Has Come Before:
Protests in History

Sometimes a protest, even a well-planned and well-run protest, can be brought to its knees by things purely outside of anyone's control. On June 19, 1968, the Poor People's Campaign, started by the Reverend Dr. Martin Luther King Jr., marched on Washington to demand that Congress take action to help eliminate poverty. The protesters camped out on park land next to the Lincoln Memorial. It rained for 28 of the 42 nights of the protest, turning the park into a near swamp and destroying the temporary shelters erected by the protesters. Because of that and poor management by protest organizers, the protest population dropped from 2,600 to 500 within ten days, and the police were able to easily move in and arrest the few that remained in place on June 24th. The protest failed to have any lasting impact.

Chapter Sixteen
How to Make a Protest Sign

One key feature of almost any protest is a good protest sign. Many of the people who see your protest will only see it as they pass on the street, or for a few seconds on the nightly news. Having a good protest sign, one that communicates your message and brings the public to your side of the debate, can be one of the most important tools you have to create change. Here are a few tips on how to make a good protest sign.

Materials

In a pinch you can scrawl your message on cardboard with a magic marker, but if you plan ahead and create your signs in advance you can have quite a bit more impact. When making your sign you want to plan for three things: mobility, durability, and visibility.

If you have to keep your sign raised high as you march you want to use lightweight materials such as heavy cardboard, signboard, or lightweight wood. Even if the signs will be in one place, keeping them light will make it easier if you need to move them. If you have time to build your signs in advance, try holding them up for a few hours. Walk around with them. If you wear out quickly, you may want to get a lighter sign.

While you want to keep the signs portable, they also have to be able to stand up to the rigors of a protest. There is nothing sadder, and few things that will reduce your impact more, than signs that are drooped over, blowing away in the wind, or so wet with rain they are illegible. You can use wooden dowels in an X shape for support, laminate the sign to keep off rain, make sure you use markers or paint that won't run, and use material heavy enough to stand up to a high wind. Some signs can be built with two handles, held by two people, for additional support. Avoid masking tape or glue for holding things together, instead opting for duct tape, staples and twine or yarn ties. Once you have your sign built, throw it around a bit. Toss it down the stairs. If it holds up, it is ready to go.

Your Message

Of course, all this work is meaningless if no one can see and read your sign. You have to make sure people can see your sign from a distance, and that a quick glancing shot by the television cameras will give you enough time to get your message across. Each message will be unique to your own protest, but there are some basics universal to all protest signs. First you want to keep your message short, ideally just a few words. A sign that reads, "Monsanto's genetically engineered food must be kept out of school lunch" is less effective than a sign that reads, "Stop Poisoning Our Children!"

Visuals are also important. What you write must have impact, but humans are visual creatures and respond to images. A sign saying that the oil industry spills 10,000 gallons of oil a year can be greatly enhanced with a picture of oil-soaked seals or birds. Hand-drawn images work in many cases, and you can print large-scale color photos on a large plotter at your local Kinko's. Once you have your message down you want to make sure it can be seen. Take your sign out and look at it from across the street. Look at it from down the block. Turn it and see if it can be read if you aren't right in front of it. And when in doubt, make it bigger.

One thing to think of when selecting a photo to use for your sign is how the media will respond to it. If you carry your sign on the streets of the city you may be able to get it in front of a few hundred people. If you get it on CNN you get it in front of millions, and there are some signs that the media simply won't point a camera at. Using the example of abortion foes, an image of an aborted fetus may stir debate and change minds, but it is not getting on the evening news. Does this mean don't use the sign? Of course not. But you need to make sure that you have plenty of signs that you can get in front of the news cameras, and that the people you want talking to the press are visually going to help your cause.

Variants

In addition, you can do quite a lot more than just a simple sign on a stick. Wider, two-person banners can be very useful at the front of marches as a sign for people to follow. These are usually better made out of cloth, which is flexible enough to let you move and turn easily but not as fragile as paper. You can sew different colors of cloth together to create signs, paint on light cloth, or even just staple cloth together. One trick that has been used is to make a Velcro backing and Velcro letters so you can slap up a good-looking banner quickly.

Another good way to carry a sign while saving your hands is to make a sandwich board, two signs held together with straps that let you wear them over your body, one in front and one in back. If you build this with some padding on the shoulders you can display your signs without tiring yourself out holding them up, and keeping your hands free to wave flags, hold bullhorns, or whatever is needed.

In the end even scrawled pen-on-paper signs may serve your needs, but if you plan ahead of time your signs can dramatically increase your impact.

Chapter Seventeen
Personal Risk Assessment

Protest is inherently risky. Confrontation and change bring with them all sorts of risks, and everyone involved on all sides needs to understand what they are getting into. By engaging in active protest you expose yourself to risk, and you should find your limits, find the lines you don't want to cross, ahead of time. If you do this you can find ways to be effective for your cause within your limits. It is too late to decide you don't want to go to jail when the handcuffs are closing on your wrists.

156

Risk comes in many forms. Ideally everyone involved should have decided where they stand in regard to these risks, but at the very least you should ensure that everyone organizing your protest has done so. Here are some of the risks you run when trying to change the world.

Risk of Personal Injury

This is a big one. When protesting you open yourself up to all sorts of physical risk, from the extreme use of tear gas, police batons, or overzealous counterprotesters to such mundane risks as heatstroke. You may not be able to fully control every risk, but by knowing where your lines are, you can stay as safe as you choose to. Not willing to get tear-gassed? Then listen to those police orders to disperse. Unwilling to get in a brawl? Don't blockade in front of angry loggers.

There is nothing wrong with not wanting to get hurt. You can help create change and never leave your home. But people willing to place themselves at risk can also change the world. One man chose to stand in front of a tank in Tiananmen Square in China, knowing full well it could roll over him without even slowing down. That image haunts the Chinese government to this day.

Risk of Jail Time

Many protests either are illegal or can wind up that way. Even with all the permits and permissions you can still be arrested. Even if you are in the right you may be arrested by cops taking an "arrest everyone and let the justice system sort it out" attitude.

Many people come to protests expecting to spend the night (at least) in jail. Many would rather not see the inside of a jail cell. Either is fine, but if your willingness to take risk does not include gray bars then you should avoid the more blatantly illegal protests.

Risk to Your Job/Job Options

This can be a less obvious risk to protests, but one you have to take into consideration. If you take to the streets to protest for something your employer or the state takes poorly, it can be held against you. This is a clear risk in strikes, but is also present in other protests.

People marching for gay rights have lost promotions or been fired by employers who feel they no longer convey the right "corporate image." Someone protesting the U.S. drilling proposal in the Alaska National Wildlife Refuge may be told they no longer have the "proper interests" to work for a legal firm that contracts for oil companies. Many people have simply been fired with no explanation. Even if you are in the right this can leave you with no recourse but long, emotionally draining lawsuits.

This may not be a huge risk for you, but depending on how controversial your issue is and where you work, you may want to think about it.

Risk to Others

You are not the only person involved in your protest. If you are asking others to march with you in the streets you are putting them at risk. They should be making this risk assessment themselves, and if they are unwilling to take the risks, they shouldn't come, but the fact remains that they are at risk. If something happens to them (say, an aggressive cop with a billy club) you may feel (and be) somewhat responsible. If you aren't willing to ask people to take risk, and if you don't feel you'll be able to live with yourself if they get hurt, then don't ask them to join you.

What Has Come Before: Protests in History

Some people are willing to take direct action, risk and all, in order to indicate their displeasure. In 1980, as part of the on-going Swords to Plowshares protests, Peter DeMott entered the General Dynamics Electric Boat Shipyard in Connecticut to protest U.S. nuclear development. Finding a security van with the keys still in the ignition, he took the van and used it to ram repeatedly into the rudder of the USS *Florida* nuclear submarine. He was able to put a good size dent in the submarine's rudder before finally being dragged out of the van and subdued. He was jailed for one year for criminal mischief and trespass.

Chapter Eighteen
Spin Control:
How to Deal Effectively With the Media

Perhaps the single most important factor in determining the effectiveness of your protest will be how and when the media gets involved. On your own you cannot hope to reach more than a handful of people; with the news cameras you can reach millions. Many aspects of your protest, from timing to costuming to location, are dramatically affected by how you want the media to see you. In many cases whole protests are designed solely as a media spectacle to get attention and get the message of the protest to the public. No matter why and how you are protesting, the media are critical to your plans. But how do they work? How can you get them on your side? Here are some tips on how to deal with the media for maximum effect.

First off, the media are so important to your effectiveness that it is usually to your advantage to have one person acting as a media liaison whose only job is to make sure reporters have everything they need and that the cameras always have someone they can point at to get your side of the story. Your target will often have entire departments of people whose only job is spin control, so having your own voice in the mix is a must.

Once you select the person to be the media liaison make sure they have all the facts, background, and information relating to your protest. It is unlikely the media is going to want every little fact (print reporters fight for every column inch of space, and television is even more limited) but by having everything organized you ensure you can give the media both whatever they need and what you want them to have. If you have time consider putting together a press pack with printed information in detail that you can hand out to reporters.

The most common way you will be communicating information to the media will often be via a press release. Some people spend four (or more) years in college in programs dedicated basically on how to write a good press release, but the basics can be mastered relatively easily. The first step is to get the fax number or e-mail address (faxes are usually preferred) for the news editor of the media outlet you are talking to. Some papers or stations will have a specific events editor or other person you may want to talk to instead, but as a default the news editor is the way to go.

You then have about two lines to get the attention of the editor and convince them that your protest is something they need to cover. You can go into some detail about your issue if it's warranted, but editors can get literally hundreds of press releases a day, and if a quick skim of the first lines doesn't get their attention they will never read down to the rest. The basic idea is to include the who, what, when, where, why, how of the issue, and go into the details later.

You also need to include as many ways to contact you to get more information as you have (e-mail address, phone, fax if you have it, and so on) so that they can get a reporter in touch with you. You might send something like:

FOR IMMEDIATE RELEASE
July 4th, 2003

University students to rally this Saturday outside the downtown federal building to protest FBI arrests

Over the past weeks the FBI has been systematically violating the rights of US citizens and legal immigrants by questioning and detaining people without warrants and without trial. On Saturday the 5th outside the steps of the federal building in downtown Seattle students of the University of Washington are staging a rally to support those held by the government and to insist that these people be given access to lawyers and their names released so the public knows who is held. Several hundred people are expected to join the students, and the rally will run from noon until midnight. Speeches will go until dusk, and a candlelight vigil will be held on the steps of the federal building to show solidarity with those held. Police response is expected.

For more information contact:
Sally Marshal
Free Our Friends
www.Freeourfriends.org
Freeourfriends@u.washington.edu
Phone (555) 237-9354
Fax (555) 237-9300

####

You want to give them both the information they need and the impression that you are committed and professional enough to deliver on what you are saying. For an event such as the one above, after sending the media this press release, you would also want to call anyone who hasn't already sent a news team (have the numbers lined up ahead of time) to inform them of breaking news (when you get started, when the cops show up, when the tear gas hits, and so on). An editor who might not send a news team to what was billed as a peaceful rally with a few dozen people might reconsider if hundreds of people show up and the cops start arresting everyone.

In addition to just keeping the media informed of your activities you may find it to your benefit to tailor your activities to fit the way the media operate. Know when reporters' deadlines are. If the eleven o'clock news sets up its nightly lineup at 3 and you don't talk to them until 5 then there almost has to be blood on the streets to get them to change their plans. If the reporters for the morning paper have to have their stories in to their editors at 8 pm and your protest starts at 7:30 you can expect light or no coverage. If you move your event to 5 or 6 you give the reporters at least some time to work. For major developments (mass arrests, dramatic violence) papers may hold the presses, but the more you can do to work within the time frame the media is working under, the more coverage you can expect.

Finally, don't feel you have to limit your interaction with the media to just the reporter who's covering your protest, or to just the day you march in the streets. If you find a reporter who gives you good coverage, who seems sympathetic to your cause, cultivate them. Get them anything they need for their stories — facts, quotes, and interviews, whatever. A good relationship with key reporters can help out immensely over the long term as you run other protests.

Look also to other parts of the paper. Letters to the editor can serve as a great tool for getting your message out before your protest and getting your view of the results out afterward. A few well-worded letters to the editor ahead of time can double the size of your protest, and can help explain your cause to people after the fact.

Overall the media should be a key element of any protest, and the time and energy you devote to cultivating relationships with them, learning what they need and delivering it, will pay off in a greatly enhanced reach for your message and effectiveness for your protest.

Chapter Nineteen
Paying for It:
Fundraising and Resources
for Your Protests

You can change the world with nothing more than a good pair of shoes and a loud voice, but many protests require quite a lot of resources. Phone bills, signs, flyers, and bail can all add up, and you will often be going up against targets with much deeper pockets. You can bankroll your protest yourself, but you can do more good if you aren't worried about going bankrupt in the process.

The first step in fundraising is to determine how much you need. Different protests take different amounts of money, and your options for what you can do may be restricted by your finances. Write up a projected budget for your protest, remembering to allow for unforeseen costs, and see how much you need.

The first place to look for money is within your own group. Figure out how much you have to work with, and see if people can chip in for basic costs. If you have a group that meets regularly you might have dues (say, five bucks a month) to create a pool of money to cover expenses. If you have a large group of people or are dealing with a large amount of money you might want to open a bank account to help keep track of donations and expenses. (On the other hand, remember that bank account records can be subpoenaed. They put Al Capone away for tax evasion.)

Once you know how much you have to work with you can start to look to outside sources of funding. There are two forms of funding you should be looking for: money and resources.

There are a number of ways to get small sums of money from donations from your local community, from setting up donation jars at events to going door to door and asking. Basically, every time you contact someone regarding your issue you have the opportunity to make a pitch for a few bucks to help cover costs. You can also set up tables in front of local stores or other public places, both to raise public awareness and raise a few bucks. This is not going to generate thousands of dollars, but should give you the tools to run small-scale or inexpensive protests.

For protests on a larger scale that require much more money you need to look outside your group and local donors for funding. If you are active over a long period of time and have clear, specific goals, grants are one option to fund protests of all types. Grants are available in all sizes, from a few hundred dollars to many thousand, and may prove to be the best way to fund large-scale protests. This process takes time, and if you need to move quickly or act in quasi-legal or illegal ways it won't work, but if you have the time grants can fund protests on a very large scale. One way to improve your ability to collect grants and other donations may be to incorporate as a non-profit organization.

Finding a grant suited to your protest requires quite a bit of legwork. Check out your local library and research online for groups dedicated to your cause, ask others who have run protests and work on your cause, and stay at it until you find the money you need.

Another way to "fundraise" is to keep your costs down. Be honest about what your costs are going to be. Offices may help you centralize your protest work but if the rent kills you your protest ends before it starts. Don't commit to offices, equipment, paid staff, or any other expense unless you can commit to paying for them.

Your local community will also prove to be a great source of funds and resources for your work. If you can present your goals in a clear, quick way to businesses and groups in your community, many may make donations of money or services. The fastest way to reduce your costs is to look at how you can get your needs met with resources supplied within your community. Need to copy 500 flyers? You may find a local copy shop that will let you copy them free or at a discount. Need to provide food for a meeting or public speech? Perhaps there's a local restaurant that will donate food. Always remember to

168

give those who donate to your cause all the thanks you can. (For example, if a restaurant donates food, place menus or business cards around for people to take.) With a little thought and a lot of footwork you can run your protest on very little actual cash.

On the subject of footwork one important thing to keep in mind when raising funds for your protest is that time is money. Every hour you spend raising money is an hour you aren't spending fighting for change directly. If it takes five people ten hours each to put on a fundraiser that raises 300 dollars, that may cover your costs, but it took 50 person hours, so you've raised only $1.60 per person hour. That's less than minimum wage. Fundraisers can do more than just bring in money (they make great community networking tools) but you want to stay focused and spend as much time and energy on your protest as you can. Stick with what got you angry in the first place.

Chapter Twenty
Things that Hurt Protests

Protests are complex events. From one person with a bull-horn to hundreds of thousands boycotting a racist restaurant chain, every protest is dynamic, and many things can go wrong. Some of them are beyond your control. If the cops choose not to honor your permits, or your corporate target flies into a different airport there may not be much you can do. But there are many things that can go wrong that are under your

170

control, things that you can do to destroy (or greatly hamper) your protest even before you get off the ground.

Choosing the Wrong Target

Any issue worth protesting is going to be fairly complex, with many different people taking many different parts. One thing that can hurt your protest is targeting your efforts at someone other than the person or entity that is really responsible. If you are aghast that your local schools serve meat supplied by the lowest bidder and want to require schools to offer more healthy options you may want to get a collection of parents together and picket the school board, or get the PTA to organize a phone bank to call the state department of education. But if the purchasing decisions are made by the city council in their annual budgets then you are barking up the wrong tree, directing all your effort at someone who cannot create the change you want.

Before you start any protest, ask yourself, "Who am I targeting here? Can they do want I want done? Is there someone who has more control or authority I should be talking to instead?" Ask yourself, "How can this person give me what I want?" Understanding what you want from your target helps ensure you stay focused on the right target and stay focused on your goals.

Not Having a Clear Goal

Many things are going to make you angry, and angry enough to demand change, but if you don't go into a protest with clear goals you're wasting your energy. Continuing the above example, if you want to improve the health value of school lunches you have to have a clearer goal than just "Our kids need better nutrition."

Imagine that you get your way instantly, that as soon as you speak with your target they immediately say, ok, we agree with you, what do we do? If all you can say is "Make lunches healthier," you don't have anything to offer. If you can say, "Offer vegetarian meals and soy milk, which you can get from these three companies, here are the price sheets and menus," you can have real impact.

Not Getting the Media Involved

The eyes of the media (and thus the public) can be one of your most powerful allies when you are trying to change the world around you. For everything from corrupt government officials to profit-over-everything corporations, the light of day can prove fatal to quite a few inhuman acts. In addition, the media can serve to protect you and your people. If you tell off the cops, they will be tempted to show you six new uses for a nightstick. If CNN is pointing a camera at you they are much more likely to stay in line and behave legally.

You should alert the media as far in advance of your protest as is feasible, unless you are planning your actions to be a surprise. At the very least you must alert the media as you move into action, and for longer protests you should keep them informed of what's going on. If the media has no information, or only the information provided by your target, your coverage will be nonexistent or worse. With the media on your side you have a better shot at generating favorable public opinion and putting additional pressure on your target to change. Many protests, such as boycotts, are almost impossible without the media involved.

Do your homework before you protest. Know what the contact numbers are for your local media, prepare press releases before you go into action, and make sure they can contact someone if they want additional information for a story. Then keep them up to speed as events develop. Cops moving in? Your target suing you? Let the media know.

Lack of Protest Follow-Up

Action is valuable, and the protest energy can get you going, but you need to do more than just act. Whether you get what you wanted or not, you need to follow up with your target, with the people protesting with you, with the media, and with the public. In success, take your bow; if you didn't get what you wanted you may be able to use your follow-up communications to lay the groundwork for further protests (or inspire others to action). If you don't do any follow-up you risk leaving your target a window to slide back through and ignore any promises they made to get you out of their lobby.

Poor Contingency Planning

Protests are dynamic events, and no one can plan for every contingency, but you must at least think through what can happen, what your target can do to marginalize you, what can go wrong, and find ways to work around or deal with these events.

Think like your target for a moment (even if you have to take a shower afterwards). If you are trying to raid a corporate meeting, what will the secretaries do to slow you down? Move the meeting location? You can prevent that by raiding just as the meeting starts. But what if they try to seal off the area before the meeting starts? Maybe you should have some people in place ahead of time to let you in (perhaps posing as delivery persons). If you plan to chain yourself to the doors and a fire starts, then what?

Make a game of it, sit around in a group ahead of time and throw out ideas for what could happen. Let people take turns pretending to be the target and thinking up ideas to shut you down. Think up things that can go wrong. You can't prepare for everything, but by thinking things out ahead of time you can negate a lot of your target's options before they can even use them.

Not Having a Sense of History

If something has you mad enough to act, to get out in the streets and protest, odds are it has pissed someone else off before you. No action takes place in a void. If you don't look at what has gone before, what else has been done regarding your issue, you risk at best being less than effective and at worst wasting yours and others' energy trying something that's been done before.

By doing your homework and learning what has gone before, you can build on it. If you target a large corporation for polluting your local waterways your case is much stronger if you can point to lawsuits they've lost for polluting in other areas. If you plan to march to protest police brutality you need to know the record of brutality of your local police force, the facts of each case, as well as a look at other protests both in your area and nationwide. If the local cops have always responded to protests with lawsuits, you approach them one way; if they always respond with tear gas, you approach from quite a different angle. Study your history or become it.

Burning Out Early

Protests take a lot of work. Fighting for change is hard. Fighting the status quo is hard. Different protests will take different amounts of time and energy but all of them take a lot of work and if you don't pace yourself you risk burning out, losing your steam and collapsing before your goals are met.

The best thing you can do to avoid burnout is to be aware that it can happen. If you try to do everything yourself, if you try to do everything too fast, if you let your anger overwhelm your planning ability, expect to burn out. By working with others, spreading out the work needed to run a successful protest, and staying focused, you can get the results you want without giving yourself a heart attack in the process.

What Has Come Before: Protests in History

In 1997, Hong Kong ended ninety-nine years of British rule and once more hoisted the flag of China. The people of Hong Kong, long used to freedoms under the British system (press freedoms, rights to assemble, rights to criticize the government), worried that the Chinese government would not honor the terms of the deal, which called for a "one country, two systems" policy. The concern was that the Chinese government would feel obligated to crack down.

Even years after the handover, the worst fears of the public appear to have been overblown. Annual protests commemorate the anniversary of the massacre in Tiananmen Square, and the Falun Gong movement, banned in China, practices in the open. So are the people's rights safe? Maybe not. Government officials have attended (otherwise legal) marches to tell protest organizers that the sound equipment in their trucks violated ordinances and could not be used without risking fines and arrest, and a popular spot used by Falun Gong to gather was blocked when the government put in a large flower planter.

No one, maybe not even the Chinese government, knows if these are just the work of a large, ponderous government or deliberate attempts to discourage and disrupt active protest. It's impossible to know for sure, but the Chinese hardly have a strong record of tolerating dissent.

Chapter Twenty-One
With Friends Like These...:
Zealots and the Over-committed on Your Own Side

Any issue important enough to protest, important enough that after trying to change things via normal channels (and failing) you have to say, no, this must change, any issue like this creates strong emotion. That emotion is going to run at different temperatures in different people, and is going to inspire different action. Some will be willing to write a letter, make a phone call, but nothing more. Some will be willing to march in the street, rally, and lead protests. And then there are some who will go over the top, who will want massive, large-scale action quickly, who want results that are very broad and far beyond the existing state of the world. These extremists can bring valuable energy, but they can also bring protests down by discrediting the participants and distracting the media.

An example: Many people are concerned about logging companies cutting down old-growth forests and replacing them with cookie cutter rows of trees that do not support wildlife. This is a legitimate issue to get concerned about, but the results people want to see vary. A protest might try to increase public awareness of what happens to the forests after the logging companies are done, or on pressuring government to apply (and enforce) new laws, or any of a number of other options. But if someone comes to the protest stating that the solution is to fully disband the logging companies, put them out of business, fire everyone involved and ban access to the deep forests, if they bring that view and get much of the news coverage, most of the air time, they color your whole effort with the brush of extremism, of a group unwilling to offer compromise or live in the "real" world, and your whole protest can easily be dismissed as out of touch and irrelevant. You could have hundreds of people in the streets, you could have a well thought-out protest representing a wide range of opinions on the issue, but if the extremists are the main voice you will have a very difficult time creating change.

There are a number of problems and difficulties in dealing with these people, not the least of which is that they are on your side. These are your allies, people willing to join in your cause and feeling (very strongly) that change is necessary.

That energy and willingness to participate is something you have to respect, but the difficulties come when they do not recognize what effect their goals have on the overall situation. Sometimes demanding great change is important, but most change happens in steps, and asking for everything at once can result in no change at all.

If those holding extremist views are not aware of how the mainstream will view their demands, and if they are both unwilling to back down and unwilling to stay somewhat quiet then you are in the uncomfortable position of needing to deal with people on your own side who can disable your protest and hurt your cause. So what do you do? How do you create change even with these "allies" shouting in your ear?

First off, if you encounter these people ahead of time (at planning meetings, at other events, and so on) you can try talking to them and pointing out the effect their views have on the overall protest. Remind them that you are all working toward the same overall goals, but that it may be better to get the ball rolling, to get some change, some action, than to try to get everything all at once. Some will agree with you, and lend their energy and power to your protests, and some will not listen. Extremists are, after all, extreme.

You can use that extremism as your next argument for keeping them out of the limelight of your protests. Continuing the logging example, those who believe the logging companies simply have to go away may be more comfortable, and more useful, torching bulldozers and spiking trees rather than marching on Washington. Legality and risk become big issues here, but change often takes actions on many different levels, and only the most extreme cannot find a way to play a productive part. In the Israel-Palestinian conflict some Palestinians are at the U.N. lobbying for change, some are in Washington, D.C., to speak with the U.S. government, asking for pressure on Israel, and some are strapping themselves with dynamite and blowing themselves up as human bombs. Whether the latter is an acceptable action in international conflict is an open debate, but the level of extremism clearly varies. All of these people color the conflict, and it remains to be seen which will ultimately create the most change.

Another, less pleasant way to deal with those whose views are too extreme is to keep them out of the protest in the first place. If you are running a protest where there is not a lot of publicity ahead of time you can try to "solve" the problem of extremists by simply cutting them out of the communications loop and not telling them what you are doing ahead of time. This is the protest equivalent of taking your ball and going home; if they won't play nicely, they don't get to play at all. This is unfortunate, in that the energy and concern they have is both valuable and valid, but it may be the best way to show the news cameras opinions more representative of your overall goals.

But what do you do when these don't work (or aren't options) and the extremists are at your protest? How do you keep the overall protest focused on your goals without being distracted by arguments over how far is too far to go?

One thing to do is to acknowledge that these people have every right to their concerns, but to try to keep their voice as one small voice in many. If you can't keep them completely off camera and away from the press (either by keeping them away from the media or keeping the media away from them) then you have to have moderate voices sounding off around them and trying to give reporters a broad view. Remember that the press, and especially the television cameras, wants a good image. You have to make sure the extremists are not the only image of your protest that the public sees. Also, try not to argue on camera. You need to avoid the media having the impression your protesters are unable or unwilling to work together.

It is important to recall that one of the best ways to bring down a protest you do not agree with is to join them, and then take such an extreme view that the whole protest is rendered useless. If you encounter someone whose view seems over the top you may want to do some checking and see if they are being funded or led by your opposition.

Overall, different types of protests require different levels of commitment. Someone who might be too extreme for a letter writing campaign might be just right for a blockade. Someone you consider a moderate may be viewed (and reported) as a fanatic by your target or sympathetic media. You, yourself, will almost certainly be labeled an extremist at some point. Remember that almost everyone has a place in the act of creating change, that each person's view is valid at least to himself, and that ultimately we are all on this planet together. One main value that extremists bring to a cause is that by looking so out there, so over the top and irrational, other protests that might have been labeled extreme now look moderate, even rational and reasonable by comparison. Organizations such as Earth First! conduct many campaigns (such as the campaign to eliminate all logging of any kind on public land) knowing that while they are unlikely to get their way the act of their protest makes groups like the Sierra Club seem much more mainstream, and gives such moderate groups a louder voice in public debate.

Chapter Twenty-Two
Your Rights and the Powers of the Police
or
So Now We Are Going to Jail

Everyone in a free society should know, and be willing to assert, their rights. As a protester and activist you are almost certainly going to come into conflict with the authorities. At some point in many protests (e.g., blockades) you are clearly behaving illegally. With some (e.g., letter campaigns) you are

184

less likely to even see your target, let alone a cop. But much of the time there will be a gray area and the legality of your actions may be in question. In addition, if your actions are antagonizing someone (and if not, then what's the point?) you can expect them to want the cops to make you go away.

This section is not intended to be definitive legal advice, and it's written from the standpoint of laws in the United States of America. You should do your homework on your local laws ahead of your protest, and know your rights before you need them.

That said, here are some things to think about when dealing with the cops.

The only universal rule of dealing with the cops (and protests in general) is DON'T PANIC. If you flip out you are much more likely to do something that is going to get you in trouble, and that is much more of a problem when dealing with police. Stay calm, think about what you are doing, and you will be in a much better position to assert your rights.

Unless you have a clear reason for doing so, do not antagonize or argue with the police. They may not be on your side, but they are (usually) just people doing their jobs, and it won't help anyone, especially you, to get into a shouting match with them. Similarly, never run from the police. You can be arrested for suspicion of illegal activity, and nothing makes you look more suspicious than running from the cops. Never touch a cop, in any way. Doing so can be construed as assault and is the fastest ticket to the back of a patrol car.

Never sign anything. With the exception of a ticket given while you are driving, you cannot be required to sign anything, and should not do so without the advice of a lawyer.

Your interaction with the cops can take many forms.

The cops have the power to stop you and ask questions.

You are under no obligation to answer any question asked by the police. You are not required to present identification or tell the police your name or any other information if stopped on the street, even if accused of (or caught in the act of) a crime. Even if placed under arrest you cannot be required to identify yourself to the police (but you may be required to do so by a judge). The exception comes if you are stopped driving (not just riding in) a car, in which case you can be required to provide your license, insurance and proof of car registration.

The cops have a limited power to search you without a warrant.

If they suspect you may be carrying a concealed weapon police have the right to stop and search you. The search is limited to items that feel like or may be weapons, and all legal non-weapon items must be returned to you after a search. If you are stopped in your car the police have the right to search your car if they have probable cause to think that a crime has been committed. In either case NEVER consent to a search and make it clear that you do not consent to any additional searches. DO NOT RESIST the police (you can be arrested for doing so), but make it clear to them and as many witnesses as possible that you are not consenting to any searches.

The cops have the power to arrest you.

That, after all, is one of their primary purposes. If you are placed under arrest you must be told what you are accused of. If you are not under arrest you are free at any time to walk away. If you are uncertain as to your status, ask the officer involved if you are under arrest. If you are, ask what you are being charged with. If not, you are free to leave and should do so if you are uncomfortable continuing to deal with the police. If you are arrested you have the right to contact a lawyer, your family, a bail bondsman, or other party. Your contact with a lawyer may not be legally monitored by police, but other communications may. Once under arrest your phone calls and letters to or from anyone other than your lawyer can (and will) be monitored.

The cops have the power to lie to you.

And they will do so if they feel it will help them get information they want. They can threaten to arrest you or those you are with. They can attempt to convince you to talk with them with lies such as, "It will go easier for you if you cooperate." The police have no authority to cut deals. Only the district attorney or prosecutor can cut deals, and only if it gets to that point. Always remember that anything you say can be used in court. Cops can make demands, play dumb and ask questions, and make incorrect or misleading statements hoping you will correct them. Until you are arrested you are usually better off not saying anything. Once you are arrested your best course of action is to STAY QUIET. If arrested you should immediately request a lawyer and say nothing else until you can get advice from a lawyer. Local lawyers can be found in your local phone book, and if you plan ahead you can get more legal information from the National Lawyers Guild (www.nlg.org).

Whenever you deal with the police you should get the badge number and vehicle patrol number of any cops you deal with (they are required to give you this information). Write down everything you can about your interaction with the cops as soon as you can, while the memory is still fresh in your mind. If you are arrested or involved with the police in front of witnesses try to get the names of some witnesses. For large protests it may be helpful to have some of your people serve as witnesses, not breaking any laws in order to watch what the cops do and get information from other witnesses.

If you are going to get arrested you should try to get arrested on camera in front of as many reporters and cameras as possible. Not only will this tend to keep the cops calmer than they might otherwise be, it also helps get your message to the public and show your commitment. Someone getting dragged off in handcuffs makes great news footage.

The American Civil Liberties Union provides a printable flyer ("Bustcard") listing your rights. It can be handed out to your fellow protesters and carried for use if you are stopped. This can be downloaded from the ACLU Web site at www.aclu.org. For your convenience we have printed the contents of the "Bustcard" below and on the following pages.

What to do if you're stopped by The Police Bustcard

Be **polite and respectful**. Never bad-mouth a police officer.

Stay **calm** and in control of your words, body language and emotions.

Don't get into an argument with the police.

Remember, **anything you say or do** can be used against you.

Keep your hands where the police can see them.

Don't run. Don't touch any police officer.

Don't resist even if you believe you are innocent.

Don't complain on the scene or tell the police they're wrong or that you're going to file a complaint.

Do not make any statements regarding the incident. Ask for a lawyer immediately upon your arrest.

Remember **officers' badge & patrol car** numbers.

Write down everything you remember ASAP.

Try to find **witnesses** & their names & phone numbers.

188

If you are injured, **take photographs of the injuries** as soon as possible, but make sure you **seek medical attention** first.

If you feel your rights have been violated, **file a written complaint** with police department's internal affairs division or civilian complaint board.

KEEP THIS CARD HANDY!

IF YOU HAVE A POLICE ENCOUNTER, YOU CAN PROTECT YOURSELF.

---

1. What you say to the police is always important. What you say can be used against you, and it can give the police an excuse to arrest you, especially if you bad-mouth a police officer.

2. You don't have to answer a police officer's questions, but you must show your driver's license and registration when stopped in a car. In other situations, you can't legally be arrested for refusing to identify yourself to a police officer.

3. You don't have to consent to any search of yourself, your car or your house. If you **DO** consent to a search, it can affect your rights later in court. If the police say they have a search warrant, **ASK TO SEE IT**.

4. Do not interfere with, or obstruct the police — you can be arrested for it.

IF YOU ARE STOPPED FOR QUESTIONING

1. It's not a crime to refuse to answer questions, but refusing to answer can make the police suspicious about you. You can't be arrested merely for refusing to identify yourself on the street.

2. Police may "pat-down" your clothing if they suspect a concealed weapon. Don't physically resist, but make it clear that you don't consent to any further search.

3. Ask if you are under arrest. If you are, you have a right to know why.

4. Don't bad-mouth the police officer or run away, even if you believe what is happening is unreasonable. That could lead to your arrest.

IF YOU'RE STOPPED IN YOUR CAR

1. Upon request, show them your driver's license, registration, and proof of insurance. In certain cases, your car can be searched without a warrant as long as the police have probable cause. To protect yourself later, you should make it clear that you do not consent to a search. It is not lawful for police to arrest you simply for refusing to consent to a search.

2. If you're given a ticket, you should sign it; otherwise you can be arrested. You can always fight the case in court later.

190

3. If you're suspected of drunk driving (DWI) and refuse to take a blood, urine or breath test, your driver's license may be suspended.

IF YOU'RE ARRESTED OR TAKEN TO A POLICE STATION

1. You have the right to remain silent and to talk to a lawyer before you talk to the police. Tell the police nothing except your name and address. Don't give any explanations, excuses or stories. You can make your defense later, in court, based on what you and your lawyer decide is best.

2. Ask to see a lawyer immediately. If you can't pay for a lawyer, you have a right to a free one, and should ask the police how the lawyer can be contacted. **Don't say anything without a lawyer**.

3. Within a reasonable time after your arrest, or booking, you have the right to make a local phone call: to a lawyer, bail bondsman, a relative or any other person. The police may not listen to the call to the lawyer.

4. Sometimes you can be released without bail, or have bail lowered. Have your lawyer ask the judge about this possibility. You must be taken before the judge on the next court day after arrest.

5. Do not make any decisions in your case until you have talked with a lawyer.

IN YOUR HOME

1. If the police knock and ask to enter your home, you don't have to admit them unless they have a warrant signed by a judge.

2. However, in some emergency situations (like when a person is screaming for help inside, or when the police are chasing someone) officers are allowed to enter and search your home without a warrant.

3. If you are arrested, the police can search you and the area close by. If you are in a building, "close by" usually means just the room you are in.

We all recognize the need for effective law enforcement, but we should also understand our own rights and responsibilities — especially in our relationships with the police. Everyone, including minors, has the right to courteous and respectful police treatment.

If your rights are violated, don't try to deal with the situation at the scene. You can discuss the matter with an attorney afterwards, or file a complaint with the Internal Affairs or Civilian Complaint Board.

Produced by the American Civil Liberties Union.

Copyright 2003, American Civil Liberties Union.

Reprinted with permission of the American Civil Liberties Union, www.aclu.org

Chapter Twenty-Three
Protesting in 24 Hours or Less

Many protests are huge events requiring cooperation between many organizations and hundreds of hours of planning. However, sometimes events move so fast that swifter action is needed. You may have gotten this book as a present, or picked it up on a whim, leafed through it and tossed it on a bookshelf and forgotten about it. Then the U.S. government invades some Third World country (again) and you need to get into the streets quickly. Or your local high school expels a group of students for not complying with a dress code and you want to get them back in classes immediately. Or your local chemical plant is shown to be leaking chemicals into local streams and every minute they continue to do so dumps hundreds of gallons of toxins into your community. Then, when speed is of the essence, you pick up this book off the shelf (or out from under the table leg) and look for how you can get going quickly. Here's how to set up and execute a protest in 24 hours or less.

Step One: Know What You Want to Do

Your first step is to identify your goals. You should be able to state both what has pissed you off and what you want done about it, and each should take no more than one clear sentence. Take a look at the chapter on goals for help here. The important thing is not to let high tempers and hot blood blind you to the need to have clear goals. If you don't have your problem and goal down to one sentence each then relax for a moment, step back and work on that first. If you go off half-cocked you risk wasting energy (yours and others) and not having the impact you want. Spending a few moments here will save you hours later.

Step Two: How Do You Want to Do It?

There are some ways to protest that lend themselves to a quick setup. To be specific, picket lines can be put together quickly, and tend to be the best protest type to run if you are trying to get set up and in place quickly. Most of this chapter will look at picket lines. Blockades can require very little time to set up (and in fact may require quick action to be effective at all) but you may have little time to do the risk assessment blockades require, and marches can be hard to coordinate on short notice.

The biggest thing that will decide what kind of protest to run is visibility. It will often be best to select a highly visible point and set up a picket line so that people can easily find and join you, you can get your message across to your target, and you can avoid the complications of large or mobile protests. Select your protest location for visibility and access, so that people can find and join you. A public street outside city hall or corporate headquarters tends to be a good choice.

Step Three: Get Your Gear

In a pinch you can protest with very little, but some equipment is going to be needed no matter what your situation. The most critical thing you will need is a sign, in order to communicate your message quickly and visually to passers-by and the media. You can drop by any local supermarket and pick up a pack of colored markers and some cardboard (they will probably give you boxes you can break up if you ask). If you have time you can also find an art supply store and pick up thicker white cardboard sheets or other poster-making material, as well as spray paint, street chalk, and other gear. At a minimum you need the following:

- ☐ Sign material (cardboard, whiteboard or other material)
- ☐ Markers, spray paint or other tools for making signs
- ☐ Cell phone(s). If you can get into position swiftly and use a cell to handle much of your other needs you can be effective faster.

Step Four: Getting People There

One person holding a sign can make a point, but a few hundred people holding signs looks much more impressive. While you are on your way to your target protest site call your friends who will be affected or may be interested in joining you. Even if they can't join you themselves they can call their friends, who can call their friends, and so on. Even in the absence of anyone coordinating the planning this can get a lot of people to your target very quickly.

In addition, you (or someone you call) should contact the media as soon as you have enough information to give them. Call them up (getting their numbers from information if you are calling while on the move) and give them your two-sentence issue and goal, and where your protest is setting up. If your issue is of local interest or particularly timely you may be able to get airtime, and once you set up your protest itself they should be told where they can send reporters. A few words on the drive-time radio can get you quite a few people out supporting your cause.

Of course, the most important person you should concern yourself with getting there is you. Almost all your calls and publicity can be done as you move into position yourself.

Step Five: Make Your Point

Once you are in position, the media is alerted, you have people coming in to help you and your target has to deal with you, all that's left is to make your point, and make it stick. The rest of this book should help you with that.

What Has Come Before:
Protests in History

The AIDS crisis blindsided many members of the traditional medical community. ACT-UP (the AIDS Coalition to Unleash Power) has a long history of raising awareness about AIDS and the needs of AIDS victims. ACT-UP/Chicago worked to get the Cook County Board of Commissioners to establish a woman's AIDS ward at the Cook County Hospital. When the Board would not agree to create such a ward, ACT-UP took to the streets.

In cooperation with other protest organizations, ACT-UP placed 16 beds, wrapped in sheets with AIDS slogans, in the middle of a busy intersection and blocked traffic, laying in the beds and refusing to move as symbolic AIDS victims. Over one hundred protesters were arrested. The AIDS ward was opened the next day.

The End?

In the end it is up to us all to explore the world, to be aware of what is going on around us and to think of how we feel about that. Events of the world move quickly. From governments starting wars that could kill millions to just wanting to ensure our children are breathing clean air, there will always be more things worth protesting. Only you can know your heart, know your mind, and know what you want to change. Choose well, plan well, and act with all your heart and you

200

can create the world you dream of. We will never live in a world free of conflict, nor should we want to. Whenever people feel strongly about an issue protest can, when combined with other actions, serve as the single best way to create change. Think. Envision the world you want to live in. Now use the tools provided here, and the energy and fire of your desire, to create that world.

YOU WILL ALSO WANT TO READ:

☐ **10065 HOW TO HIDE THINGS IN PUBLIC PLACES, *by Dennis Fiery*.** Did you ever want to hide something from prying eyes, yet were afraid to do so in your home? Now you can secrete your valuables away from home, by following Dennis Fiery's eye-opening instructions in *How to Hide Things in Public Places.* The world around us is filled with cubbyholes and niches that can be safely employed... and this book identifies them. Among the topics covered are: How can you possibly hide things in public places?; Principles of public hiding; Containers, dead drops and miniatura; Landscape and hiding around the home; The street and other urban areas; Hiding items with innocent bystanders; Public buildings and businesses; Some specific public buildings to consider; Relaying messages; Some safety rules; And much, much more! Illustrated with numerous photographs. *1996, 5½ x 8½, 216 pp, illustrated, soft cover. $15.00.*

☐ **94281 101 THINGS TO DO 'TIL THE REVOLUTION, Ideas and resources for self-liberation, monkey wrenching and preparedness, *by Claire Wolfe*.** We don't need a weatherman to know which way the wind blows — but we do need the likes of Claire Wolfe to help grease the wheels as we roll towards the government's inevitable collapse. "Kill your TV... Join a gun-rights group... Fly the Gadsden flag... Buy and carry the Citizen's Rule Book... Join the tax protestors on April 15... Buy gold, guns, and goodies..." Wolfe's list is lengthy and thought-provoking, as she elaborates on each piece of advice. From generalities to precise instructions, her 101 helpful hints cannot be ignored or disregarded, if one is truly serious about becoming more self-sufficient in preparation for a major societal change. For the concerned citizen who wishes to keep a low profile, protest his or her rights and survive the "interesting times" which are sure to come, this is essential reading. *1996, 5½ x 8½, 196 pp, soft cover. $15.95.*

☐ **94304 DON'T SHOOT THE BASTARDS (YET), 101 More Ways to Salvage Freedom, *by Claire Wolfe*.** The clodhoppers of Tyranny stomp on the toes of innocent people every day, from flat-out prohibitions of peaceful activities, to flagrant invasions of privacy, to the not-so-subtle erosion of Constitutional freedoms. But it's still not time to take down the scoundrels. Not yet. Author Claire Wolfe has come up with another batch of ideas to counteract the abuses government and private agencies so routinely practice. In this follow up to her wildly popular *101 Things to Do 'Til the Revolution*, she provides more ways to monkey wrench a system that keeps citizens in a stranglehold. She teaches how to prepare for a truly independent lifestyle, and imparts further insight on how to liberate people from the Powers that Be. You can wax on about freedom. You can whine about government rules. But the only way to change the way things are is to take action against the Tyranny traipsing all over American lives. This book is the best place to start. *1999, 5½ x 8½, 239 pp, soft cover. $15.95.*

☐ **88220 THINK FREE TO LIVE FREE, A political burnout's guide to life, activism and everything,** *by Claire Wolfe.* This is a workbook for anyone who cares about principles and causes yet has become burned out and exhausted by their activism. It is for those who have reached the point where that nagging feeling, telling them their passions have been blighting their personal lives rather than enriching them, is their constant companion. Anyone who has acted on their desire for social change rather than just wished for it to happen and has seen their commitment pull apart everything that feed their soul should read this book to find out how to get their lives refocused in the direction they want to be going. Life-long activist Claire Wolfe has designed worksheets to help you pinpoint the activities you do that defeat your true purpose and help you discover what the true purpose is. These worksheets will help you determine what activities are useless time wasters, and how to focus on behaviors and habits that help you accomplish your true goals. *2001, 8½ x 11, 124 pp, illustrated, soft cover. $14.95.*

☐ **19209 OUT OF BUSINESS: Force a Company, Business, or Store to Close Its Doors... for Good!,** *by Dennis Fiery.* When filing a formal complaint, asking for your money back, and engaging in healthy competition just doesn't do the trick, you need to take serious action. This book arms you with 101 ways to derail, deflate, and destroy your target business. And if you want to protect your own business, this book is the best insurance policy you'll ever buy. The author gives new meaning to the term "corporate downsizing" in this revenge treatise. *Sold* *for information and entertainment purposes only. **1999, 5½ x 8½, 298 pp, soft cover. $17.95.***

☐ **19212 21ST CENTURY REVENGE, Down & Dirty Tactics for the Millennium, *by Victor Santoro.*** The bad news: Technology has opened the door to a slew of modern revenge methods never before possible! Master revenge writer Victor Santoro explains how to turn technology to your advantage in the art of revenge. In this book you will learn: how to protect yourself from caller ID, and how to make it work for you; how to turn political correctness into political chaos; why your target's garbage can be his undoing; how the Internet is your world-wide resource for revenge. This book not only shows you how to form the ultimate revenge plan, but also how to protect yourself from those seeking revenge on you! ***1999, 5½ x 8½, 150 pp, illustrated, soft cover. $15.00.***

*We offer the very finest in controversial and unusual books — A complete catalog is sent **FREE** with every book order. If you would like to order the catalog separately, please see our ad on the next page.*

SBH3

LOOMPANICS UNLIMITED
PO BOX 1197
PORT TOWNSEND, WA 98368

Please send me the books I have checked above. I am enclosing $ _____ which includes $6.25 for shipping and handling of orders up to $25.00. Add $1.00 for each additional $25.00 ordered. *Washington residents please include 8.2% for sales tax.*

NAME _____

ADDRESS _____

CITY _____

STATE/ZIP _____

We accept Visa, Discover, and MasterCard. To place a credit card order *only,* call 1-800-380-2230, 24 hours a day, 7 days a week.
Check out our Web site: www.loompanics.com